Quilting, Sewing & Appliqué
Essential Techniques for Beginners

Learn the Fundamentals and Build Your Creative Skills

HEIDI PRIDEMORE

Landauer Publishing

Quilting, Sewing & Appliqué: Essential Techniques for Beginners

Landauer Publishing, www.landauerpub.com, is an imprint of Fox Chapel Publishing Company, Inc.

Copyright © 2025 by Heidi Pridemore and Fox Chapel Publishing Company, Inc.

All rights reserved. No part of this book may be reproduced, stored in a retrieval system, or transmitted in any form or by any means, electronic, mechanical, photocopying, recording, or otherwise, without the prior written permission of Fox Chapel Publishing, except for the inclusion of brief quotations in an acknowledged review and the enlargement of the template patterns in this book for personal use only. The patterns themselves, however, are not to be duplicated for resale or distribution under any circumstances. Any such copying is a violation of copyright law.

Project Team
Acquisitions Editor: Amelia Johanson
Editor: Christa Oestreich
Designer: Wendy Reynolds
Studio Photographer: Mike Mihalo
Proofreader & Indexer: Jean Bissell

Photo on page 12 courtesy of BERNINA of America.
Photo on page 13 (top left) courtesy of Oliso.
Shutterstock used: Elovich (wood background: front cover [middle], 26–27, 65, 87); HAKINMHAN (background: front cover [bottom left]).

ISBN 978-1-63981-100-7

Library of Congress Control Number: 2025934183

To learn more about the other great books from Fox Chapel Publishing, or to find a retailer near you, call toll-free at 800-457-9112 or visit us at www.FoxChapelPublishing.com.
You can also send mail to:
Fox Chapel Publishing
903 Square Street
Mount Joy, PA 17552

We are always looking for talented authors. To submit an idea, please send a brief inquiry to acquisitions@foxchapelpublishing.com.

Note to Professional Copy Services:
The publisher grants you permission to make up to six copies of any quilt patterns in this book for any customer who purchased this book and states the copies are for personal use.

Printed in China
First printing

MIX
Paper | Supporting responsible forestry
FSC® C016973

This book has been published with the intent to provide accurate and authoritative information in regard to the subject matter within. While every precaution has been taken in the preparation of this book, the author and publisher expressly disclaim any responsibility for any errors, omissions, or adverse effects arising from the use or application of the information contained herein.

Introduction

Welcome to *Quilting, Sewing & Appliqué: Essential Techniques for Beginners*, where every stitch brings creative positivity to life! Whether you're picking up a needle for the first time or looking to expand your sewing expertise, this book is designed to guide you step-by-step through projects that not only teach essential skills, but also inspire your imagination and sparks creativity.

    We start with the beautiful blocks that you can take on individually. Once you've mastered the techniques, you can create fun projects or even turn them into a full-size quilt designed for its inspirational messaging. The blocks aren't just lessons—they're creative prompts that will encourage you to experiment and make something uniquely yours. There is something here for quilters of every age and level. From sewing in zippers and working with vinyl to mastering the art of fusible appliqué, this content is crafted to help you build confidence as you go. The goal is simple: to equip you with a diverse set of techniques that will open a world of possibilities in your sewing journey. Let this guide be your companion as you explore new techniques, refine your skills, and create pieces you'll be proud to call your own.

    You'll notice, too, that very beginners can select solid fabrics to focus on the learning process, so as not to stress about mixing and matching prints, whereas more skilled readers might want to expand their possibilities trying out prints and coordinates. Where a printed fabric option is pictured, the yardages are listed in one of two ways: either adjacent to the solid yardages or in a separate sidebar with any additional construction information required. You'll see too that I've pictured the quilt in bright solids and a selection of pretty prints. It's amazing how a simple change in fabric results in something completely different.

Happy sewing!
Heidi

> **Look out for QR codes throughout the book, leading to expanded techniques, walk-throughs for each project, and ideas for bonus projects!**

28

45

35

48

55

51

63

Contents

Terms-to-Know Visual Glossary 6
Tools and Supplies to Gather 12
Basics Techniques to Master 21
Piecing the Blocks 27
   Imagine Block 28
   Inspire Block 30
   Sun Block 33
   Laugh Block 35
   Butterfly Block 38
   Large Daisy Block 42
   Create Block 45
   Smile Block 48
   Dream Block 51
   Hearts Block 55
   Starburst Block 58
   Stars Block 61
   Mini Daisies Block 63
Making Pretty Projects 65
   Imagine Bench Pillow 66
   Sun Fabric Baskets 69
   Laugh Table Runner 73
   Dream Pocket Pillow 76
   Starburst Zipper Pouch 80
   Mini Daisy Pincushion 85
Putting It All Together 87
   Building the Quilt Top 88
   Making the Quilt Sandwich 94
   Quilting the Quilt 97
   Binding the Quilt 98
Templates 102
Acknowledgments 125
About the Author 126
   About the Tech Editor 127
Index 128

Terms-to-Know Visual Glossary

If you're an absolute beginner, and even if you have some experience, it can be helpful to learn or review quilting, sewing, and appliqué terms before diving in. With this visual glossary, you won't only learn these terms, you'll see what each looks like. Words in *italics* are defined elsewhere in the glossary. Descriptions of tools and materials used throughout this book are found on pages 12–20.

Learn more basics with my Beginner Quilting Series videos!

APPLIQUÉ
Appliqué is when a piece of fabric, generally a fabric motif or specific shape, is prepared and stitched to a base fabric. See page 24 for the fusible appliqué technique. Here, the appliqué motif is applied with a *satin stitch*. You'll also see straight-stitch (*raw-edge*) and *blanket-stitch* appliqué in this book.

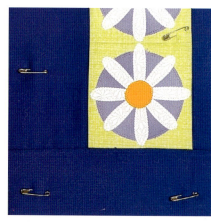

BASTING
The process of temporarily securing the *quilt sandwich*. This step is crucial in preventing the fabric from shifting and puckering during the *quilting* process. There are three common basting techniques: pin basting, inserting safety pins every few inches; spray basting, using a temporary adhesive spray; thread basting, using long, loose stitches. Each method has its advantages, with pin basting being widely used for durability, spray basting for quick application, and thread basting for hand-quilting projects.

BINDING
Strip or strips of fabric that covers the raw edge of a quilt to finish it (see page 96). When finished, binding is generally ¼" (6.4mm) or ½" (1.3cm) wide.

Quilting, Sewing & Appliqué: Essential Techniques for Beginners

BLANKET STITCH

This stitch finishes raw edges, often being used to secure an *appliqué* to a base fabric. The stitch travels horizontally along the raw edge then bites vertically into the appliqué in every other stitch. For the purposes of this book, our blanket stitch is done by machine.

BLOCK

Blocks, also known as quilt blocks, refer to the separate units joined together to make a larger quilt or project. Blocks can be one single square or rectangle, or they can be built with several smaller units. They can be *pieced* or *appliquéd*.

EDGE STITCH

When you're instructed to edge stitch, you will be topstitching a row of stitching just along the very edge of your project. Generally, you wouldn't edge stitch more than ⅛" (3.2mm) from the edge.

FAT EIGHTH

A fat eighth is fabric, which is cut similarly to a *fat quarter* but only measures 9" x 22" (22.9 x 55.9cm). It is still an ⅛ yard (11.4cm) of fabric, but this rectangle is cut crosswise rather than on the grain.

FAT QUARTER

A fat quarter is fabric, which is cut from the crosswise grain of a ¼ yard (18" x 44" [45.7 x 111.8cm]) rectangle, yielding an 18" x 22" (45.7 x 55.9cm) rectangle. It is sometimes called a "Fat Quarter yard."

HALF-SQUARE TRIANGLES

The half-square triangle, abbreviated to HST, is a square unit made by joining two triangles together (see page 21). An HST can also be made with two squares or four squares that are joined and cut diagonally. This yields two or four equal-size HSTs, depending on the technique.

Terms-to-Know Visual Glossary

INTERFACING
Thin or cushioned product made of polyester that is attached to the *wrong side* of fabric to reinforce and prevent stretching. Can be sewn or adhered with heat.

LONG ARM QUILTING
Quilts the layers (*quilt sandwich*) of a quilt together using an industrial long arm machine. The technique is similar to *machine quilting*, which uses a home sewing machine instead. Long arm services are available at quilting and sewing machine shops for a fee.

MACHINE QUILTING
Stitching through layers of fabric with a sewing machine.

NESTING SEAMS
Pressing intersecting *seam allowances* to the right and left (opposite of one another) to better allow the fabric to lay flat.

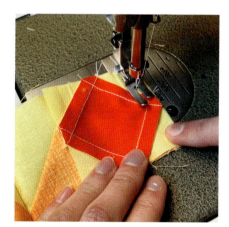

PIECING
Sewing together small fabric shapes to create a pattern (see page 23).

PRECUTS
Fabrics cut to specific sizes and sold by fabric manufacturers, often in bundles of coordinating colors or prints. Some of these common sizes are *fat quarters* and *fat eighths*.

8 Quilting, Sewing & Appliqué: Essential Techniques for Beginners

PRESS

Press with an iron. This can be to iron fabric flat or adhere an *appliqué* with fusible web to fabric. Most commonly, this refers to ironing the *seam allowance* flat. When instructions say to press seams, this means to press them open; the directions will state if the seams need to be pressed in another manner.

QUARTER-INCH SEAM ALLOWANCE

Most quilting projects call for a ¼" (6.4mm) seam allowance—as opposed to garment sewing, which generally calls for a ½" (1.3cm) or ⅝" (1.6cm) seam allowance. It's essential to test and practice your ability to sew a consistent ¼" (6.4mm) seam when piecing for patchwork, so that your seams align properly.

QUILT BACK

Traditionally, a whole piece of cloth. As shown here, two joined pieces can create a quilt back. The back should be made or cut larger than the *quilt top*, 8" (20.3cm) all around, because the *quilting* process may gather the fabric and reduce the overall size.

QUILT SANDWICH

A *quilt top*, batting, and *quilt back* fabric. These three layers are required to finish any quilt.

QUILT TOP

A created length of fabric for the face of a quilt or quilted project. Often consisting of *blocks*, rows, columns, *sashing*, and borders.

QUILTING

Process of sewing together a *quilt sandwich*. Quilting can be simple lines, but a common technique is to sew designs like swirls and spirals. It is usually the next-to-last step, completed before *binding*.

Terms-to-Know Visual Glossary

RAW-EDGE APPLIQUÉ
Another technique for finishing appliqué. Rather than using a *satin stitch* or *blanket stitch* to hide the edges, a straight stitch is used ⅛" (3.2mm) from the edge, leaving them raw. The fusible web technique should protect the edges from fraying.

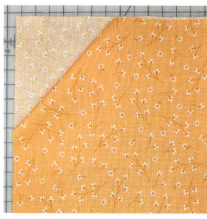

RIGHT SIDE
The front of the fabric; most noticeable when the fabric has a print.

ROUGH CUT
Cutting around a motif (like a *template*) outside the drawn line about ⅛" (3.2mm). Templates are usually rough cut before adding the product to the fabric. Once added to fabric, the template is cut on the drawn line. This two-part cutting assures that the glue will cover the entire motif.

SASHING
Pieces of fabric that separate *blocks* or rows of blocks on a *quilt top*.

SATIN STITCH
This stitch finishes raw edges and is often used to secure an *appliqué* to a base fabric. The stitch travels in a tight zigzag along the fabric edge to cover it with a solid width of stitching.

SELVAGE
The finished edges on woven fabric. They are generally cut off and discarded before using fabric for a project.

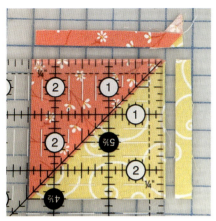

SQUARE UP
The process of lining the vertical, horizontal, and diagonal lines on a clear quilt ruler (generally a square one) with your sewn unit or *quilt block* underneath, in order to cut an exact size. Tracing paper and straight rulers can also be used.

STITCH-IN-THE-DITCH
A *quilting* technique where you sew directly in the join of a seam. It emphasizes the seam and secures the quilt without interfering with the design.

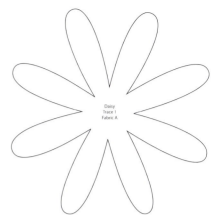

TEMPLATE
A pattern used for the design or motif you plan to *appliqué*, embroider, or *piece*.

WHIPSTITCH
A stitch used for joining one piece of fabric to another by sewing one edge over the other with small stitches.

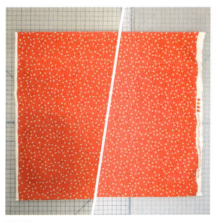

WOF
Width of fabric is abbreviated to WOF. Most quilt cottons are 44" (111.8cm) wide. Shown here is a splice of each end. When directions say to cut a strip or piece a certain length by "WOF," it means 44" (111.8cm) wide.

WRONG SIDE
The back of the fabric; most noticeable when the fabric has a print on the other side (*right side*).

Terms-to-Know Visual Glossary

Tools and Supplies to Gather

In this section, we are covering the supplies needed for this book. Each project lists the specific supplies needed, but here we will go into more details about these supplies and cover any additional information you may need. You can always reference this section as you start each project if you have any questions about the materials needed.

▍ Basics Supplies for Quilting, Sewing, and Appliqué

"Basic sewing supplies" is listed on many quilting and sewing patterns without much explanation. This is because experienced sewers understand what this includes. In this section, we will list what is usually included in this tool kit and what each one is.

SEWING MACHINE

The number one requirement for sewing and quilting is a sewing machine in good working order. My recommendation is to purchase the best machine you can afford. If you try to sew on a poor-quality machine, you're going to end up frustrated. Beginners don't need a top-of-the-line computerized embroidery model, but they should invest in a quality brand-name machine with adequate room in the throat area. Some brands to consider include BERNINA, Baby Lock, Brother, Elna, Husqvarna-Viking®, Janome, JUKI, PFAFF®, and SINGER.

Consider looking for models that are designed specifically for quilters, which will include a wider work area and specialty feet.

Sewing machines have multiple interchangeable feet that are used for different techniques. They vary from machine to machine, and additional presser feet can be purchased for specialty sewing or quilting purposes. I recommend an open-toe presser foot for appliqué (see page 16).

IRON AND IRONING BOARD

Invest in a quality steam iron. Once you sew together two pieces of fabric, pressing the fabric piece open is essential. Press your quilt units and blocks well and often. If you get in the habit of pressing all your pieces as you sew, you will find things will line up better and the finished piece will look much nicer. Always press in a lifting pressing motion; do not iron back and forth when quilting or appliquéing, as it can stretch or distort your pieces.

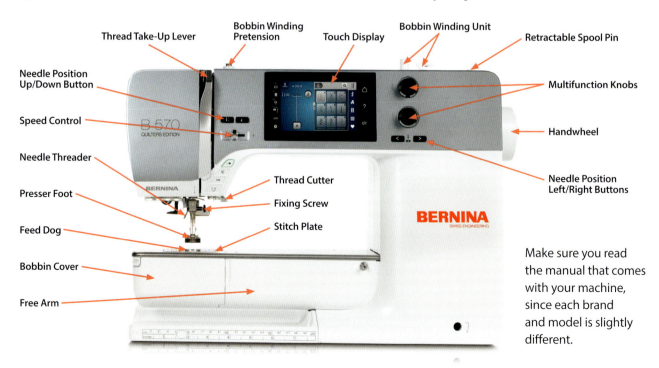

Make sure you read the manual that comes with your machine, since each brand and model is slightly different.

Quilting, Sewing & Appliqué: Essential Techniques for Beginners

An ironing board or mat absorbs heat better than other work surfaces, which could be damaged.

Select an ironing board for durability with height adjustments. If you're lucky enough to have an older ironing board, they were often constructed with materials that have stood the test of time. You want a board that is sturdy enough to withstand pressing and moving large quilts over the surface without tipping. Make sure your cover has a pad underneath and fits tightly; replace if it becomes torn or scorched. Scorch marks can transfer to your projects with heat.

Since ironing is a major step in sewing and piecing, I recommend having an ironing station near the sewing machine. This can be a standard-size iron and ironing board or just a travel iron and a small mat for pressing. The larger set up is easier to use when assembling the quilt, but most of the projects in this book can be made with the smaller iron and mat.

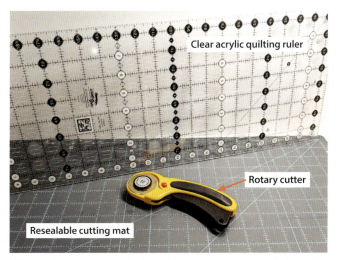

While scissors can do the job, these three tools are beloved by quilters and make every project much easier.

ROTARY CUTTER, ACRYLIC RULER, AND CUTTING MAT

For patchwork and quilting, rotary cutters are extremely helpful for cutting uniform fabric units. A rotary cutter, always with a sharp blade, results in clean-cut edges. This tool can be extremely sharp, so be careful when using it. **Always engage the safety guard when the rotary cutter is not in use.**

You need to pair your rotary cutter with a specialized, resealable mat so as not to damage the surface beneath. Consider purchasing the largest mat that you can and that suits your crafting environment, as well as a smaller mat to place by your machine, so you can quickly and conveniently cut pieces while sewing.

Ideally, pick up a collection of acrylic rulers. Those with no-slip features are best for beginners to avoid moving on the fabric when you cut. Straight, clear rulers provide an edge for guiding your rotary cutter and are a must for measuring and quilting. Square, clear quilt rulers are ideal for cutting consistent blocks (squaring up) and come in a variety of sizes.

SCISSORS

For any sewing or quilting project, you need good-quality scissors that are only used on fabric. Fabric scissors usually have 8"–10" (20.3–25.4cm) blades in length. For appliqué, you'll want a separate pair.

These are all different kinds of scissors with slightly different uses.

Tools and Supplies to Gather

Small trimmers come in handy for smaller pieces and projects, as well as for clipping threads. These would have 3"–4" (7.6–10.2cm) blades.

If you know anyone who sews, you may have noticed that they have two pairs of scissors: one pair for fabric and another for paper. This is because, when scissors are used to cut paper, the paper causes the blade to dull quickly. Cutting fabric with scissors does not affect the blades as quickly. Since cutting fabric with dull scissors is challenging, most sewers use one pair of scissors exclusively on fabric to keep the blade sharper and longer lasting.

ERASABLE MARKING PEN

There are times when we need to make a temporary mark on our fabric. A wash-away pen, chalk pencil, or iron-off pen makes this possible. Wash-away marking pens stay until you remove them with a damp cloth, so keep in mind you will need to wet your project after completion in most cases to remove a residual mark. Heat-disappearing ink pens for fabric enable you to remove markings with the heat of an iron. Since these marks disappear with heat, you'll want to make sure not to press areas where marks need to remain for sewing purposes later. Chalk pencils will naturally disappear over time.

Because each block in this book requires several units, I advise keeping whichever pen you prefer close at hand. It's important, especially for beginners, to label the units on the back side as you complete them, so you join pieces correctly. No matter which removeable marking pens you use, test them on your fabric first to make sure the marks won't remain after the recommended removal process. My favorites are a Bohin Extra-Fine Mechanical Chalk Pencil for dark fabrics and a Pilot FriXion pen for lighter fabrics.

STRAIGHT PINS AND PIN CUSHION

We often use straight pins to hold two pieces of fabric together when sewing. You will need some sharp straight pins and a pin cushion to hold them. Select pins that are easy to pick up, have nice sharp points, and in a length that is adequate for quilting. My favorite brands are Taylor Seville Magic Pins™ and Clover. Pins from both companies are very sharp and slide into the fabrics easily.

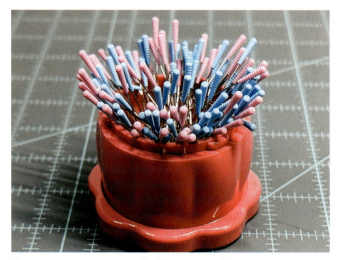

Keep your pins organized with a pin cushion or a cute cup like this one.

Tip: When using straight pins at the sewing machine: Pull the pin out of the fabric before the pieces go under the presser foot on the machine.

SEWING CLIPS

Clips can be used nearly everywhere you might pin to hold layers of fabric together for stitching. They open wide for layered projects like securing binding around a prepared quilt. The flat side lets them lie on the sewing machine base, and unlike pins, they're easy to find if dropped. There are many brands of clips on the market, but my favorite ones are Clover Wonder Clips.

TEMPORARY GLUE STICK

A wash-away glue stick may not be included in everyone's basic sewing supplies, but I find it handy when sewing a zipper to fabric. It is much easier to

Pay attention to the instructions for each pen or pencil you buy, so you know how to remove the marks from your fabric.

14 Quilting, Sewing & Appliqué: Essential Techniques for Beginners

Some people prefer to use clips more than pins. They both work, so it's all a matter of preference.

While there are temporary glues made for fabric, I find this school brand works just as well.

glue the zipper to the fabric than to try and pin or clip the pieces together. Make sure you buy a glue that is listed as water soluble, washable, or temporary.

HAND-SEWING NEEDLES

Having a package of hand-sewing needles in your basic sewing kit, such as milliners needles, is also a good idea. There are times when we have to hand sew an opening closed, instead of using a sewing machine. I recommend using the same 50-weight thread that is used on the machine for hand-sewing.

SEAM RIPPER

Sadly, there are times when mistakes are made, and the pieces have to be separated and resewn. A seam ripper is the tool for the job. It has a curved head and a sharp point. This tool slides under the threads and breaks them so the two pieces can be separated without stretching or tearing the fabric. Make sure it's sharp; dull seam rippers can distort your fabric as threads are pulled, not cut. They are sold for a couple dollars upwards to $15 and have basic plastic handles or ergonomic varieties.

Milliners needles are a good choice for hand sewing.

Everyone makes mistakes, so do not be afraid to use your seam ripper when needed.

Tools and Supplies to Gather 15

Fabrics

All samples in this book were first made using solid and tonal 100% cotton quilting fabric. This type of fabric will not fray at the edges, which is especially important when using the fusible appliqué techniques throughout the book. Tonal refers to a fabric that has different variations of the same color rather than a pure solid. After using solids and tonals, we reworked the projects in mixed prints to share the effect that fabric choices have on your results. Have fun with your fabric choices, and mix whimsical prints in with the tonal and solid fabrics to make each project your own.

The motif edges on the right side of a batik have sharper edges, but quilters use whichever side suits their design sense.

> **Tip:** When selecting any fabrics for projects with appliquéd elements, lay the two fabrics on top of each other to make sure the appliquéd elements pop off the background fabrics you have chosen.

For the solid-color-fabric projects, I used a combination of Kona Solids® from Robert Kaufman Fabrics, and tonal and weave fabrics from Benartex Designer Fabrics. The prints are a mix of quilting cottons from various vendors: Moda Fabrics, Riley Blake Designs, Kimberbell, FreeSpirit Fabrics, and more.

When you are sewing or creating appliqué effects, you'll need to be aware of the right and wrong side of the fabrics in most cases. Here are some tips based on the type of fabric you use:

- **Printed quilt cottons** generally have an obvious right and wrong side.
- **Batiks** are often an exception. For quilting purposes, batiks are abstract prints of tightly woven cotton created with a wax-resistant dye process. Depending on the density of color you're looking for, you can use either side, as there is often just a slight difference in the sharpness of the design.
- **Solid or single-color fabrics** can be more of a challenge. If you look at the selvage, it can help indicate which side is the right side. In general, the tiny holes in the selvage, which occur in fabric production, push from the wrong side out. In other words, the holes are flat on the wrong side and slightly raised on the right side. Selvages sometimes list the manufacturer's name or fabric line also. The side on which the selvage has printed text is the right side of your fabric.

What fabric you choose—prints (left), tonals (center), solids (right), or a combination—will completely change your finished project.

Holes on the selvage edge are generally flat on the wrong side (left) and raised on the right side (right).

Do note, however, if you can't tell the wrong or right side, most likely no one else will be able to tell either. Ideally, once you select a "right" side, make all pieces the same.

▮ Threads

The standard thread for sewing and quilting is 50-weight (50wt). You can also use 40wt or 28wt threads to add a pop to the edge stitching or to

Large spools of thread are available in plenty of colors to match your fabric.

Picking Thread Colors

To audition threads for your projects, pull out one thread from the spool and lay it on top of the fabric. This gives you a more accurate idea of how the thread will look on the edge of the fabric. It is also a much better way to match the thread than laying the spool on the fabric.

This pink thread does not look as bold as the spool when I'm only using one strand.

embellish the pieces with some decorative stitches. The lower the number of a thread size, the thicker the thread. A 28wt thread will be thicker than a 50wt thread. Thicker threads are often used to enhance the decorative effect. I used Aurifil Cotton 50wt threads for all the projects in this book.

Here are some tips on picking threads for the projects:

- If you are a beginner at sewing on a machine, I recommend picking thread colors that blend in with the fabrics. This will hide any imperfections that occur with beginners. Use 50wt threads for the stitching since it is a thinner thread and again will blend into the fabrics.
- If you want to experiment with thread colors on the projects, use contrasting colors for the top or edge stitching. Play with the different thread weights to add more impact. Use 40wt or 28wt threads to make the stitching pop up.

Tools and Supplies to Gather

■ Helpful Supplies for Appliqué

Most of the projects in this book are done using the fusible appliqué technique. This is a fun and easy technique that allows you to apply a fabric design on top of a piece of fabric. Here, I cover the tools you need, and on page 24, I go over the basic steps for fusible appliqué. Fusible web is an adhesive and also an important part of the technique, but I'll go over that in depth in the next section.

PERMANENT MARKER

Markers are used to trace or create the design that will be appliquéd. I recommend using a Sharpie Ultra Fine Marker. The tip on this pen is the same thickness as a scissor blade, making it easier to cut out the shapes on the drawn line. Sharpie markers will not smear on the paper, your hand, or the fabric. These markers also come in all kinds of pretty colors.

You can also use a pen and pencil, but they are typically not as visible or reliable as a marker.

APPLIQUÉ PRESSING SHEET (OPTIONAL)

An appliqué pressing sheet is a Teflon sheet that is a good base because fusible web will not stick to it. Appliqué shapes can be built and pressed together on top. Once the layered shapes are put together on the appliqué pressing sheet, you can pull the arrangement off and position it onto the fabric. It is also a good idea to use an appliqué pressing sheet on top of your ironing surface to keep the fusible web from sticking to your ironing board.

This sheet is uniquely resistant to fusible web, making it a better work surface when working with appliqué.

OPEN-TOE PRESSER FOOT

To finish the edges of the appliquéd shapes, you will need to see the edge of the fabric. An open-toe foot lets you see the stitches as they go through the fabric without obstruction.

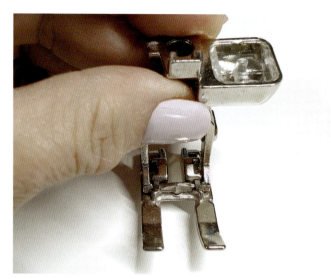

This sewing machine foot allows you to see your stitches more than other machine feet.

■ Fusible Web, Stabilizers, and More

Throughout the book, we'll use various sewing products to stabilize, fuse, or fill different projects. These products are typically available in quilt shops and sewing stores, where you can ask for them. Keep in mind that these stores often keep them behind the counter. Many of these products can be purchased by the yard, or you may find them conveniently prepackaged and ready to use.

Though many of these products look alike, make sure you use the correct item listed for each project. They are not interchangeable. Let's review these items to explain what they are and when to use them.

FUSIBLE WEB

Used for appliqué and made by various manufacturers, fusible web is a polyester product with a protective paper sheet and adhesive bond on both sides. Once applied to the wrong side of fabric with an iron, bonding the fabric and web together, the paper is peeled away to reveal a surface that can then be adhered to a separate fabric base. This product makes fusible appliqué possible.

There are many types and brands of fusible web on the market. For the projects in this book, make sure to use paper-backed fusible web. The projects in

Fusible is attached to the back of fabric by pressing with an iron and activating the glue.

the book were created using HeatnBond Lite. Other popular brands are Trans-Web and Wonder-Under®.

STABILIZERS

Stabilizer can be a permanent addition to your fabric; when applied to the wrong side of fabric, it can add body or stiffness to the finished project. Temporary stabilizers are used under your stitching to avoid puckering under appliqué and decorative stitches. Heavy fabrics, such as felt, might not need a stabilizer. Temporary stabilizers can be tear-away, wash-away, or heat-away.

When permanent stabilizer is listed for a project in this book, I used Pellon® 809 Décor-Bond®. This stabilizer is stiffer than most and has a fusible web on one side to make it easier to apply to the fabric. For the appliqué purposes in this book, I recommend a

A stabilizer is especially useful for small or odd-shaped pieces of fabric, keeping them stiff as you work.

lightweight, tear-away stabilizer that is placed under the project for stitching appliqués, then carefully torn away.

STUFFING

Stuffing is a loose-packed fiber used for stuffing pillows and stuffed animals. It can be called fiberfill, Poly-Fil®, or plain old stuffing. Stuffing can be made from polyester, cotton, or wool. I recommend using cotton or polyester filling for these projects. You can also buy cushions, called pillow forms, if you want to avoid loose material.

To fill an item, such as a pillow, pack the item with small clumps of stuffing. Pack the fiber in place a little at a time. You can use a chopstick to push the stuffing to the corners, creating a full project without lumps.

You may need to add more stuffing than you expect; fill and test as you go.

BATTING OR WADDING

This is a soft layer of material that goes between the quilt top and the backing. The batting adds warmth and weight to the quilt. Once the quilt top is complete and the backing is sewn together, we will layer and baste the quilt top, batting, and backing together (making a sandwich) before we start quilting.

Quilt batting is available in wool, cotton, or polyester. Polyester is a great choice for quilts that will be washed often, but I prefer using cotton batting because it breathes better and drapes nicely. Wool is a more expensive choice, but it is also lovely to work with.

Batting comes in different lofts, which are the thickness of the material. I recommend starting with a low-loft batting since it will make the quilt lighter

Tools and Supplies to Gather

Batting is an important part of the quilt, though is rarely seen because it sits between two layers of fabric.

and easier to maneuver under the sewing machine as you quilt the layers together.

FUSIBLE FOAM

When we want a bag to hold its shape and stand up on its own, we will use fusible foam. Fusible foam is a thin material with a fusible web applied to one or both sides.

Fusible foam is 100% sewing machine safe, passing through the machine when sewing the project together. I recommend using a walking foot, or you can use a dual-feed setting if your sewing machine has one. Fusible foam adds shape and body to projects like eyeglass cases, purses, tote bags, and more.

Fusible foam acts as a supporting layer in quilted projects.

FUSIBLE FLEECE

Fusible fleece is polyester batting with a fusible web applied to one or both sides of the material, meaning it is like fusible foam but has more of a drape to the finished project. This makes it easier to apply to fabric than plain batting, since you can iron it in place before cutting the pieces. It will also act as a stabilizer and add body to the finished piece. Since it is made from polyester, the material will not shrink when washed. This is a perfect product to use for bags, placemats, and wall hangings.

This handy product keeps the batting in place as you make the quilt sandwich for smaller quilted projects.

VINYL

Some of the projects call for sew-in vinyl, which you can get at most quilt or craft stores. Though vinyl comes in many weights, I recommend using thicker vinyl, around 8–10mm. The thicker vinyl is easier to use, adds body to the end project, and will last longer than the thinner products.

Vinyl will make your project thicker than the typical layering of fabric.

Basic Techniques to Master

The main techniques you will master as you work through this book are appliqué, making half-square triangles, and piecing. Here, we will walk through these processes so you will be able to complete each project. Refer to these basics as needed.

Learn how to sew a quarter-inch seam allowance.

Half-Square Triangle Basics

1. The most common way to make half-square triangles is to take two equal-size squares of two different fabrics. On one, draw a light pencil line from corner to corner.

2. Place the two squares right sides together with the pencil line facing up. At the machine, stitch ¼" (6.4mm) away from one side of the pencil line.

3. Turn the square unit 180 degrees. Stitch ¼" (6.4mm) away from the opposite side of the pencil line.

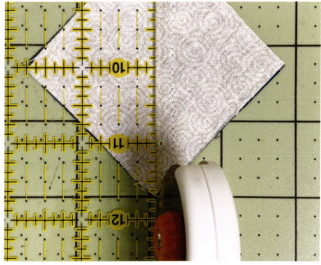

4. Using a rotary cutter and straight-edge ruler, cut directly on the pencil line. This will create two units.

Basic Techniques to Master

5. Open each unit. Using an iron, press the seam allowances to the darker fabric. **Note:** The image shows fabric pressed to the light side. Notice there are tails (tiny triangles of fabric that extend from the block) now that you have ironed the HST.

6. Trim the tails even with the HST unit. Using a clear ruler, align the stitched HST with the size square you need—for our purposes, a 2" x 2" (5.1 x 5.1cm) square HST. Square up, cutting two sides at a time with a rotary cutter until reaching the desired size.

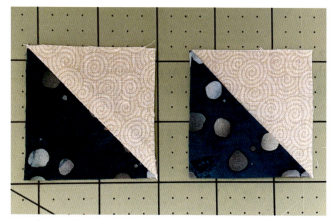

7. This technique yields two equal-size HSTs.

> ### For this Tutorial…
> To prepare for the piecing tutorial on the opposite page, make two more identical HSTs. When you get to step 5 of this tutorial, press the seam allowances to the lighter fabric instead (as shown).

▍Piecing Basics

The key to basic piecing is to make sure that you are nesting your seams. This will help your quilt top to lie flat.

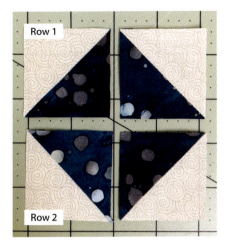

1. Using the HSTs from the previous tutorial, arrange them so that the darker sections are facing inward and the seam allowances are pressed in opposite directions from side to side and top to bottom.

2. Starting with Row 1, place the HST units right sides together as shown; the seams will nest. Stitch the HSTs together using a ¼" (6.4mm) seam allowance. Press the seam allowance to the left with an iron. Repeat with Row 2, which will mirror the first row. Press the seam allowance to the right.

3. Place Row 1 (upside down) onto Row 2 right sides together. Arrange so that the center seam allowances nest.

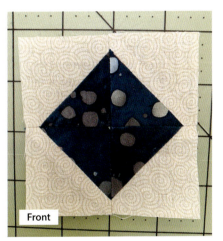

4. Stitch Row 1 and 2 together with a ¼" (6.4mm) seam.

5. Open. Press center seam open (instead of to one side or another) with an iron.

Basic Techniques to Master

Fusible Appliqué Basics

1. Trace the templates for the project onto the paper side of the fusible web. If desired, transfer all the labels from the paper templates when tracing. This will help keep all the pieces straight before they are combined into the final shape.

2. Roughly cut out each paper shape. Cut about 1/8" (3.2mm) outside the drawn lines, not directly on them. As you cut out the shapes outside the drawn lines, you can place the pieces onto the correct fabric.

> **Tip:** When you are tracing multiple pieces of the same shape, number them to better keep track of how many you have traced.

3. Place the fabric wrong side up on the ironing board. By having the fabric wrong side up at the start, it is less likely that you will accidentally press the shapes to the front of the fabric and ruin it.

4. Press each fusible web shape to the wrong side of the fabric. Follow the manufacturer's instructions that come with the fusible web.

5. Cut out each shape on the drawn lines. Since we waited to cut the shape out on the drawn lines until after it was pressed to the fabric, the edges of each shape will be sealed in glue, reducing the likelihood of the fabric edges fraying.

6. Center the shapes onto the background, and press with an iron. Follow the manufacturer's instructions for pressing time and temperature, and pay attention to the placement diagram for each project.

7. To finish the raw edges, use an open-toe foot, a decorative stitch, and matching cotton thread. The most popular stitch for finishing fusible appliqué is the blanket stitch. If your machine does not have this, chose a zigzag stitch. Or, since your edges will be "glued" to the background fabric, you can just use an edge stitch, leaving a narrow "raw" edge around your appliqué design.

> **Tip:** Please note that when you use a heavier stitch, such as a satin stitch, you need to add a lightweight, removable stabilizer to the back of the piece.

Basic Techniques to Master

Piecing the Blocks

In this chapter, we are going to build our blocks, which will let you test out your sewing, piecing, appliqué, and even your organizational skills. Make each one to join into the larger Inspire Quilt (page 87), finish as mini quilts, or use for Making Pretty Projects (page 65). See which block you might want to try for a brand-new project. You'll be brimming with confidence, and dare I say, a feeling of joy as you complete each block. Each of these patterns is designed with simple piecing or appliqué technique in mind for beginners.

Imagine Block

The Imagine Block teaches you how to use fusible appliqué by applying letters onto the fabric. You can create any word you want once you've learned the basics.

FABRIC REQUIREMENTS:

Solid—Light Blue (A)	½ yard (45.7cm)
Solid—Hot Pink (B)	Fat Quarter
Print—White Floral (C)	Fat Eighth
Solid—Bright Orange (D)	Fat Eighth

SUPPLY REQUIREMENTS:

- Imagine templates (pages 102–105)
- Fusible web
- 50wt matching cotton threads
- Basic sewing supplies and tools

CUTTING REQUIREMENTS:

Solid—Light Blue (Fabric A)
- (1) 12½" x 40½" (31.8 x 102.9cm) rectangle

Solid—Hot Pink (Fabric B)
- (1) set of Letters
- (1) "I" Dot

Print—White Floral (Fabric C)
- (2) Large Daisies
- (2) Small Daisies

Solid—Bright Orange (Fabric D)
- (2) Large Daisy Centers
- (2) Small Daisy Centers

Watch a video tutorial on this block and its project.

28 Quilting, Sewing & Appliqué: Essential Techniques for Beginners

When you reach the inner corners of the flower, feel free to pause, pick up the foot, and turn the project. This is easier than making that tight turn!

INSTRUCTIONS

1. Referring to Fusible Appliqué Basics (page 24), make the templates for the Imagine Block as listed in the Cutting Requirements. Transfer the notes on each template onto the paper side of the fusible web.

2. Roughly cut out each template about ⅛" (3.2mm) outside the drawn lines.

3. Press each fusible web template onto the wrong side of the fabric. The templates and Cutting Requirements indicate which shape goes with which fabric. Cut out each template/fabric piece on the drawn lines.

4. Arrange the pieces on the 12½" x 40½" (31.8 x 102.9cm) Fabric A rectangle. Press with the shiny side down.

5. Finish the raw edges of each shape with a decorative stitch, such as a blanket or satin stitch. Use matching threads. This completes the 12½" x 40½" (31.8 x 102.9cm) Imagine Block.

Inspire Block

The Inspire Block demonstrates how to add fusible appliqué elements to a border before attaching them to the block. Once mastered, this technique allows embellishment of any border before incorporating it into your projects.

FABRIC REQUIREMENTS:

Solid—Royal Blue (A)   ⅓ yard (30.5cm)
Tonal—Periwinkle (B)   ⅓ yard (30.5cm)
Tonal—Powder Blue (C)   ⅛ yard (11.4cm)
Tonal—Iris (D)   ¼ yard (22.9cm)
Solid—Sea Blue (E)   ¼ yard (22.9cm)

SUPPLY REQUIREMENTS:

- Inspire templates (pages 106–108)
- Fusible web
- 50wt matching cotton threads
- Basic sewing supplies and tools

CUTTING REQUIREMENTS:

Solid—Royal Blue (Fabric A)
- (2) 2½" x 36½" (6.4 x 92.7cm) strips
- (1) 2½" (6.4cm) x WOF strip. Subcut into:
  - (2) 2½" x 8½" (6.4 x 21.6cm) strips
  - (4) 2½" x 2½" (6.4 x 6.4cm) squares

Tonal—Periwinkle (Fabric B)
- (1) 8½" x 36½" (21.6 x 92.7cm) rectangle

Tonal—Powder Blue (Fabric C)
- (44) Small Scallops

Tonal—Iris (Fabric D)
- (1) set of Letters
- (4) Circles

Solid—Sea Blue (Fabric E)
- (44) Large Scallops

Watch a video tutorial on this block (and a bonus project).

INSTRUCTIONS

1. Referring to Fusible Appliqué Basics (page 24), make the templates for the Inspire Block as listed in the Cutting Requirements.

Unit 1

Unit 2 make 4

3. Center and press (1) Fabric D Circle onto (1) 2½" x 2½" (6.4 x 6.4cm) Fabric A square to make (1) Unit 2. Repeat to make (4) Unit 2 squares total. Finish the raw edges of each shape with a decorative stitch. This completes Unit 2.

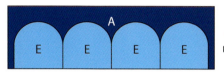
Unit 3 make 2

4. Arrange and press (4) Fabric E Large Scallops onto (1) 2½" x 8½" (6.4 x 21.6cm) Fabric A strip to make (1) Unit 3. Repeat to make a second Unit 3.

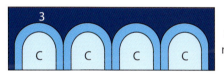
Unit 4 make 2

2. Arrange the Letter pieces on the 8½" x 36½" (21.6 x 92.7cm) Fabric B rectangle. Press with the shiny side down. Finish the raw edges of each shape with a decorative stitch. This completes Unit 1.

5. Arrange and press (4) Fabric C Small Scallops onto (1) Unit 3 to make (1) Unit 4. Repeat to make a second Unit 4. Finish the raw edges of each shape with a decorative stitch. This completes Unit 4.

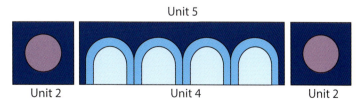
Unit 5
Unit 2   Unit 4   Unit 2

6. Sew (1) Unit 2 to each end of (1) Unit 4 to make (1) Unit 5. Repeat to make a second Unit 5.

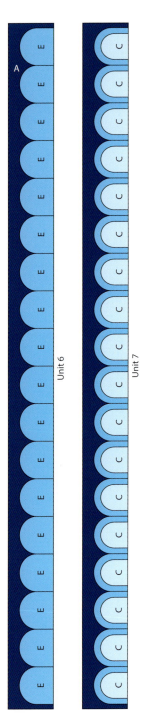

7. Just as you did for Units 3 and 4, arrange (18) Fabric E Large Scallops and (18) Fabric C Small Scallops onto (1) 2½" x 36½" (6.4 x 92.7cm) Fabric A strip. Finish with decorative stitching to complete Unit 7. Repeat to make a second Unit 7.

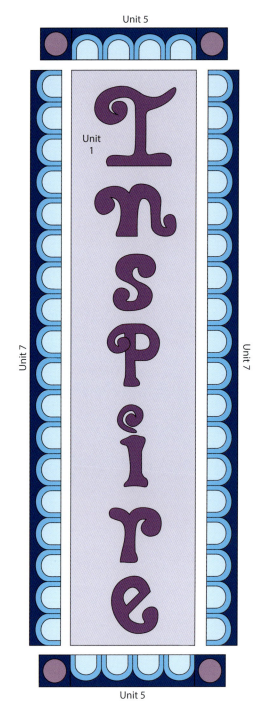

8. Sew (1) Unit 7 to each side of Unit 1. Sew (1) Unit 5 each to the top and to the bottom of Unit 1. This completes the 12½" x 40½" (31.8 x 102.9cm) Inspire Block.

Sun Block

The Sun Block is created using layers of overlapping fabric to form a sun. Learning this fusible appliqué technique is an excellent way to incorporate intricate shapes into a completed image.

FABRIC REQUIREMENTS:

Print—Orange Weave (A)	⅛ yard (11.4cm)
Print—Yellow Weave (B)	⅛ yard (11.4cm)
Solid—Pale Yellow (C)	Fat Eighth
Solid—Light Teal (D)	Fat Quarter

SUPPLY REQUIREMENTS:

- Sun templates (page 109)
- Fusible web
- 50wt matching cotton threads
- Basic sewing supplies and tools

CUTTING REQUIREMENTS:

Print—Orange Weave (Fabric A)
- (8) Outer Rays

Print—Yellow Weave (Fabric B)
- (8) Inner Rays

Solid—Pale Yellow (Fabric C)
- (1) Sun Center

Solid—Light Teal (Fabric D)
- (1) 12½" x 12½" (31.8 x 31.8cm) square

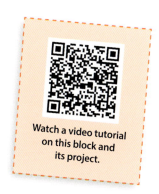

Watch a video tutorial on this block and its project.

INSTRUCTIONS

1. Referring to Fusible Appliqué Basics (page 24), make the templates for the Sun Block as listed in the Cutting Requirements.

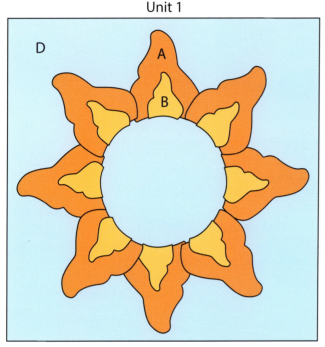

Unit 1

Unit 2

2. Arrange the (8) Fabric A Outer Rays and (8) Fabric B Inner Rays on the 12½" x 12½" (31.8 x 31.8cm) Fabric D square. Press with the shiny side down to make Unit 1.

3. Press the Fabric C Sun Center onto Unit 1 to make Unit 2.

4. Finish the raw edges of each shape with a decorative stitch, such as a blanket or satin stitch. Use matching threads. This completes the 12½" x 12½" (31.8 x 31.8cm) Sun Block.

Optional

If you have decorative stitch options on your machine, this is the perfect place to try them out. Draw a circle guideline in the Sun Center and follow the design. You'll want to practice on a test piece to determine length. Look closely and you can see another stitch for the tone-on-tone rays. Shown are stitches 40 and 16 on the Husqvarna SE, but these are popular stitches on many brands of embroidery machines.

Watch a video tutorial on this block and its project.

Laugh Block

The Laugh Block teaches you how to create a diamond border using the Triangle-in-a-Square Unit. You'll learn how to use paper templates to cut the fabric pieces. Many beautiful blocks can be made from paper templates, so this is a valuable skill to master.

FABRIC REQUIREMENTS:

Print—White Floral (A)
¼ yard (22.9cm)

Solid—Bright Orange (B)
⅛ yard (11.4cm)

Solid—Pale Yellow (C)
⅓ yard (30.5cm)

Solid—Flame Red (D)
¼ yard (22.9cm)

Print—Orange Weave (E)
¼ yard (22.9cm)

Solid—Peach (F)
½ yard (45.7cm)

SUPPLY REQUIREMENTS:
- Laugh templates (pages 110–112)
- Fusible web
- 50wt matching cotton threads
- Basic sewing supplies and tools
- *Optional:* Creative Grids® 2 Peaks in 1 Triangle Quilt Ruler

CUTTING REQUIREMENTS:

Print—White Floral (Fabric A)
- (2) Large Daisies
- (4) Small Daisies

Solid—Bright Orange (Fabric B)
- (1) 2½" (6.4cm) x WOF strip. Subcut into:
  - (18) Template 2 (T-2)

Solid—Pale Yellow (Fabric C)
- (1) 2½" (6.4cm) x WOF strip. Subcut into:
  - (36) Template 1 (T-1)
- (1) 2½" (6.4cm) x WOF strip. Subcut into:
  - (36) Template 3 (T-3)
- (1) 1½" (3.8cm) x WOF strip. Subcut into:
  - (16) 1½" x 1½" (3.8 x 3.8cm) squares

Solid—Flame Red (Fabric D)
- (1) 2½" (6.4cm) x WOF strip. Subcut into:
  - (4) 2½" x 2½" (6.4 x 6.4cm) squares
- (1) set of Letters

Print—Orange Weave (Fabric E)
- (1) 2½" (6.4cm) x WOF strip. Subcut into:
  - (18) Template 2 (T-2)
- (2) Large Daisy Centers
- (4) Small Daisy Centers

Solid—Peach (Fabric F)
- (1) 16½" (41.9cm) x WOF rectangle. Subcut into:
  - (1) 16½" x 20½" (41.9 x 52.1cm) rectangle

INSTRUCTIONS

1. Referring to Fusible Appliqué Basics (page 24), make the templates for the Laugh Block as listed in the Cutting Requirements.

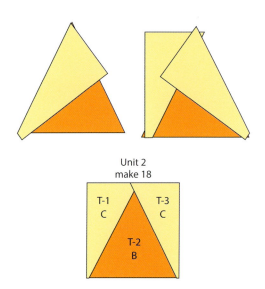

2. Arrange the Letter pieces on the 16½" x 20½" (41.9 x 52.1cm) Fabric F rectangle. Press with the shiny side down. Finish the raw edges of each shape with a decorative stitch. This completes Unit 1.

3. Place (1) Fabric C Template 1 on top of (1) Fabric B Template 2 right sides together. Align the left edges. Sew the triangles together along the left side. Press the T-1 triangle open. Repeat on the opposite side with (1) Fabric C Template 3 and the same Fabric B Template. Press the T-3 triangle open to make (1) Unit 2. Trim to measure 2½" x 2½" (6.4 x 6.4cm). This completes Unit 2. Make (18) Unit 2 squares total.

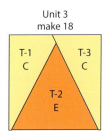

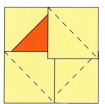

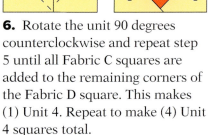

4. Repeat step 3 with (18) Fabric C Template 1 triangles, (18) Fabric C Template 3 triangles, and (18) Fabric E Template 2 triangles. This makes (18) Unit 3 squares.

5. Place (1) 1½" x 1½" (3.8 x 3.8cm) Fabric C square on the top-left corner of (1) 2½" x 2½" (6.4 x 6.4cm) Fabric D square, right sides together. Sew across the diagonal of the Fabric C square. Flip over to form a corner triangle and press. Trim away the excess fabric, cutting ¼" (6.4mm) away from the seam.

6. Rotate the unit 90 degrees counterclockwise and repeat step 5 until all Fabric C squares are added to the remaining corners of the Fabric D square. This makes (1) Unit 4. Repeat to make (4) Unit 4 squares total.

Quilting, Sewing & Appliqué: Essential Techniques for Beginners

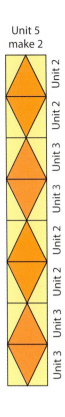

7. Arrange (4) Unit 2 squares and (4) Unit 3 squares. Sew together to make (1) Unit 5. Repeat to make a second Unit 5.

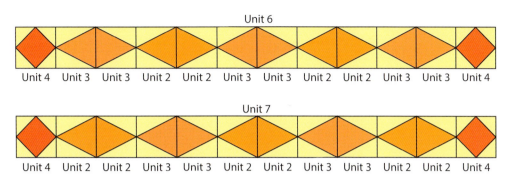

8. Arrange (4) Unit 2 squares, (6) Unit 3 squares, and (2) Unit 4 squares. Sew together to make (1) Unit 6. Repeat for Unit 7, this time arranging (6) Unit 2 squares, (4) Unit 3 squares, and (2) Unit 4 squares.

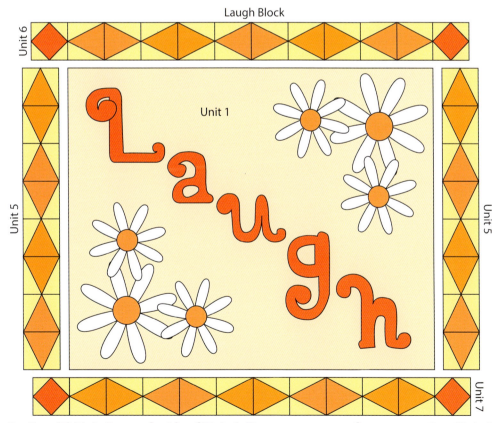

9. Sew (1) Unit 5 to each side of Unit 1. Press seams away from center. Sew Unit 6 to the top of Unit 1, and sew Unit 7 to the bottom of Unit 1. Press seams away from center. This completes the 20½" x 24½" (52.1 x 62.2cm) Laugh Block.

Butterfly Block

The Butterfly Block is created using a combination of techniques we have previously covered. The block is pieced with triangles and squares, then enhanced with fusible appliqué elements. Finally, we use strip piecing to create the checkerboard bottom.

FABRIC REQUIREMENTS:

Tonal—Rose (A)
¼ yard (22.9cm)

Tonal—Light Turquoise (B)
¼ yard (22.9cm)

Print—Yellow Weave (C)
¼ yard (22.9cm)

Solid—Bright Green (D)
¼ yard (22.9cm)

Print—Lime Weave (E)
¼ yard (22.9cm)

Solid—Sapphire (F)
¼ yard (22.9cm)

SUPPLY REQUIREMENTS:

- Butterfly templates (page 113)
- Fusible web
- 50wt matching cotton threads
- Basic sewing supplies and tools

Watch a video tutorial on this block (and a bonus project).

CUTTING REQUIREMENTS:

Tonal—Rose (Fabric A)
- (1) 6½" (16.5cm) x WOF rectangle. Subcut into:
  - (2) 4½" x 6½" (11.4 x 16.5cm) rectangles
  - (2) 2½" x 6½" (6.4 x 16.5cm) strips
  - (1) 3⅞" x 3⅞" (9.8 x 9.8cm) square. Subcut across one diagonal to make (2) 3⅞" (9.8cm) triangles
  - (2) 3½" x 3½" (8.9 x 8.9cm) squares

Tonal—Light Turquoise (Fabric B)
- (1) 4½" (11.4cm) x WOF strip. Subcut into:
  - (2) 4½" x 4½" (11.4 x 11.4cm) squares
  - (1) 4¼" x 4¼" (10.8 x 10.8cm) square. Subcut across both diagonals to make (4) 4¼" (10.8cm) triangles (there will be 2 left over)
  - (2) 3½" x 3½" (8.9 x 8.9cm) squares

Print—Yellow Weave (Fabric C)
- (1) 4¼" (10.8cm) x WOF strip. Subcut into:
  - (1) 4¼" x 4¼" (10.8 x 10.8cm) square. Subcut across both diagonals to make (4) 4¼" (10.8cm) triangles (there will be 2 left over)
  - (3) 3½" x 6½" (8.9 x 16.5cm) rectangles
- (2) Small Dots

Solid—Bright Green (Fabric D)
- (2) 1½" (3.8cm) x WOF strips. Subcut into:
  - (2) 1½" x 14½" (3.8 x 36.8cm) strips
  - (2) 1½" x 12½" (3.8 x 31.8cm) strips

Print—Lime Weave (Fabric E)
- (2) 2½" (6.4cm) x WOF strips. Subcut into:
  - (3) 2½" x 20½" (6.4 x 52.1cm) strips
- (2) Small Dots

Solid—Sapphire (Fabric F)
- (2) 2½" (6.4cm) x WOF strips. Subcut into:
  - (3) 2½" x 20½" (6.4 x 52.1cm) strips
- (2) Large Dots

Quilting, Sewing & Appliqué: Essential Techniques for Beginners

INSTRUCTIONS

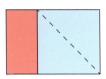

Unit 1

 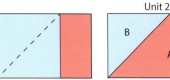

Unit 2

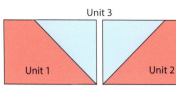

Unit 3

1. Place (1) 4½" x 4½" (11.4 x 11.4cm) Fabric B square on the right side of (1) 4½" x 6½" (11.4 x 16.5cm) Fabric A rectangle, right sides together. Sew across the diagonal of the Fabric B square. Trim away the excess fabric on back side ¼" (6.4mm) away from the seam. Press the triangle open to make (1) Unit 1.

2. Repeat step 1 with (1) 4½" x 4½" (11.4 x 11.4cm) Fabric B square on the left side of (1) 4½" x 6½" (11.4 x 16.5cm) Fabric A rectangle to complete Unit 2.

3. Sew Unit 1 to the left side of Unit 2. This makes (1) Unit 3.

Unit 5

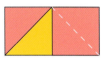 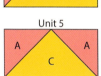

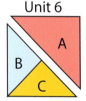 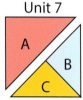

Unit 6   Unit 7

Unit 4

4. Sew together (2) 2½" x 6½" (6.4 x 16.5cm) Fabric A strips end-to-end. This makes (1) Unit 4.

5. Just as you did for Units 1 and 2, place (1) 3½" x 3½" (8.9 x 8.9cm) Fabric A square on the left side of (1) 3½" x 6½" (8.9 x 16.5cm) Fabric C rectangle, right sides together and sew across the diagonal. Trim seam allowance to ¼" (6.4mm) on wrong side and press open. Repeat with a (1) 3½" x 3½" (8.9 x 8.9cm) Fabric A square on the right side of the unit, sewing across the diagonal. Trim and press to complete Unit 5.

6. Sew together (1) 4¼" (10.8cm) Fabric B triangle and (1) 4¼" (10.8cm) Fabric C triangle along a short side. Sew (1) 3⅞" (9.8cm) Fabric A triangle to the newly sewn triangle along the long side. This makes (1) 3½" x 3½" (8.9 x 8.9cm) Unit 6 square. Repeat to complete (1) Unit 7, making sure to swap the position of the Fabric B and C triangles

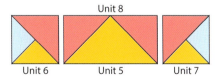

Unit 8

 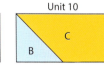

Unit 9   Unit 10

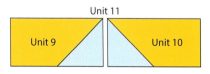

Unit 11

7. Sew together Unit 6, Unit 5, and Unit 7 in that order from left to right. This makes (1) Unit 8.

8. Just as you did for Units 1 and 2, make Unit 9 with (1) 3½" x 3½" (8.9 x 8.9cm) Fabric B square and (1) 3½" x 6½" (8.9 x 16.5cm) Fabric C rectangle. Make Unit 10 with (1) 3½" x 3½" (8.9 x 8.9cm) Fabric B square and (1) 3½" x 6½" (8.9 x 16.5cm) Fabric C rectangle.

9. Sew Unit 9 to the left side of Unit 10. This makes (1) Unit 11.

Butterfly Block

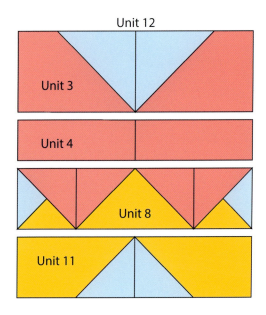

10. Sew together Unit 3, Unit 4, Unit 8, and Unit 11 as shown to complete (1) 12½" x 12½" (31.8 x 31.8cm) Unit 12 square.

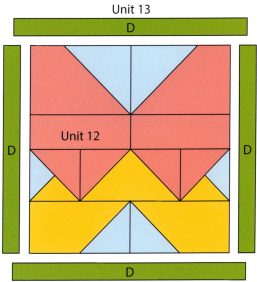

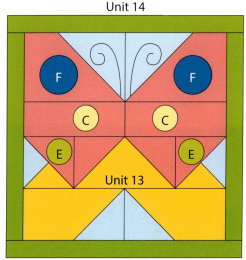

11. Sew (1) 1½" x 12½" (3.8 x 31.8cm) Fabric D strip to each side of Unit 12. Press seam allowances away from center. Sew (1) 1½" x 14½" (3.8 x 36.8cm) Fabric D strip to the top and to the bottom of Unit 12. This makes (1) 14½" x 14½" (36.8 x 36.8cm) Unit 13 square.

12. Referring to Fusible Appliqué Basics (page 24), make the templates for the Butterfly Block as listed in the Cutting Requirements.

13. Arrange appliqué dots on Unit 13. Press with the shiny side down. Finish the raw edges of each shape with a decorative stitch. Hand or machine embroider the antennas using a backstitch and black thread. This completes Unit 14.

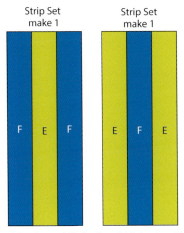

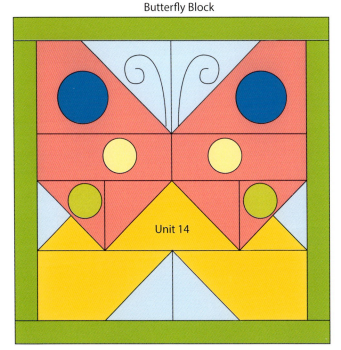

14. Sew (1) 2½" x 20" (6.4 x 52.1cm) Fabric F strip to each side of (1) 2½" x 20" (6.4 x 52.1cm) Fabric E strip. Repeat, sewing (1) 2½" x 20" (6.4 x 52.1cm) Fabric E strip to each side of (1) 2½" x 20" (6.4 x 52.1cm) Fabric F strip. This makes (2) Strip Sets total.

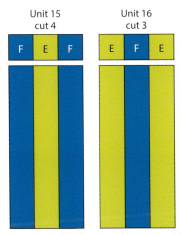

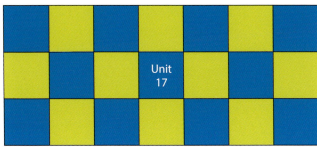

17. Sew Unit 17 to the bottom of Unit 14. This completes the 20½" x 14½" (52.1 x 36.8cm) Butterfly Block.

15. From (1) Strip Set, cut (4) 2½" x 6½" (6.4 x 16.5cm) strips to make Unit 15. From (1) Strip Set, cut (3) 2½" x 6½" (6.4 x 16.5cm) strips to make Unit 16.

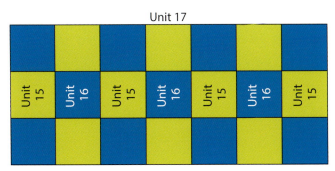

16. Arrange (4) Unit 15 strips and (3) Unit 16 strips. Sew together to make (1) Unit 17.

Butterfly Block 41

Large Daisy Block

The Large Daisy Block is a great example of how to enhance a traditional pieced block with an appliquéd daisy. Once you see how easy it is to alter the appearance of a block by adding shapes or letters with fusible appliqué, you can create any look you like. It's also a fun place to try out some decorative stitching or leave unembellished—your choice.

FABRIC REQUIREMENTS:

Print—White Floral (A)   Fat Eighth
Print—Orange Weave (B)   ⅛ yard (11.4cm)
Tonal—Periwinkle (C)   ¼ yard (22.9cm)
Tonal—Violet (D)   ⅓ yard (30.5cm)
Print—Lime Weave (E)   ¼ yard (22.9cm)

SUPPLY REQUIREMENTS:

- Daisy templates (pages 113–114)
- Fusible web
- 50wt matching cotton threads
- Basic sewing supplies and tools

CUTTING REQUIREMENTS:

Print—White Floral (Fabric A)
- (1) Daisy

Print—Orange Weave (Fabric B)
- (1) Flower Center

Tonal—Periwinkle (Fabric C)
- (1) 3½" (8.9cm) x WOF rectangle. Subcut into:
  - (4) 3½" x 3½" (8.9 x 8.9cm) squares
- (1) 2" (5.1cm) x WOF strip. Subcut into:
  - (16) 2" x 2" (5.1 x 5.1cm) squares

Tonal—Violet (Fabric D)
- (1) 5" (12.7cm) x WOF rectangle. Subcut into:
  - (4) 2" x 5" (5.1 x 12.7cm) strips
  - (1) 3½" x 3½" (8.9 x 8.9cm) square
  - (4) 2" x 3½" (5.1 x 8.9cm) rectangles
- (1) Background Circle

Print—Lime Weave (Fabric E)
- (1) 3½" (8.9cm) x WOF rectangle. Subcut into:
  - (4) 3½" x 5" (8.9 x 12.7cm) rectangles

Watch a video tutorial on this block (and a bonus project).

INSTRUCTIONS

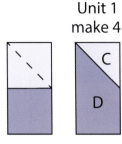

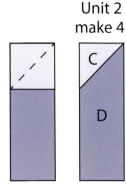

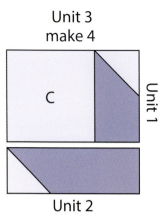

1. Place (1) 2" x 2" (5.1 x 5.1cm) Fabric C square on the top of (1) 2" x 3½" (5.1 x 8.9cm) Fabric D strip, right sides together. Align the top corners. Sew across the diagonal. Trim seam allowance on wrong side to ¼" (6.4mm) and press unit to complete (1) Unit 1. Repeat to make (4) Unit 1 rectangles total.

2. Just as you did for Unit 1, place (1) 2" x 2" (5.1 x 5.1cm) Fabric C square on the top of (1) 2" x 5" (5.1 x 12.7cm) Fabric D strip. This makes (1) Unit 2. Repeat to make (4) Unit 2 strips total.

3. Sew (1) Unit 1 to the right side of (1) 3½" x 3½" (8.9 x 8.9cm) Fabric C square. Sew (1) Unit 2 to the bottom of the unit to make (1) 5" x 5" (12.7 x 12.7cm) Unit 3 square. Repeat to make (4) Unit 3 squares total.

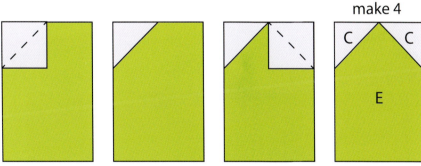

4. Just as you did for Unit 1, place (1) 2" x 2" (5.1 x 5.1cm) Fabric C square on the top-left corner of (1) 3½" x 5" (8.9 x 12.7cm) Fabric E rectangle, right sides together. Repeat on the opposite corner using (1) 2" x 2" (5.1 x 5.1cm) Fabric C square. This makes (1) Unit 4. Repeat to make (4) Unit 4 rectangles total.

Large Daisy Block

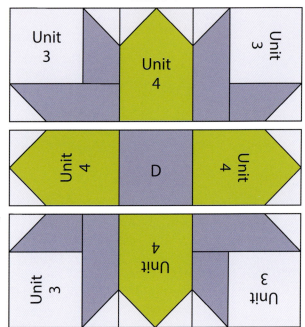

Unit 5
make 1

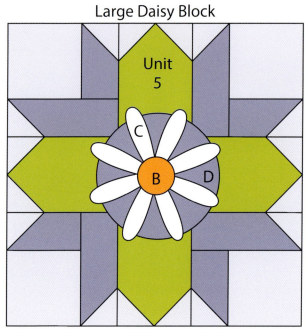

Large Daisy Block

5. Sew (1) Unit 3 to each side of (1) Unit 4 to make the top row. Repeat to make the bottom row. Sew (1) Unit 4 to each side of (1) 3½" x 3½" (8.9 x 8.9cm) Fabric D square to make the middle row. Sew together the rows lengthwise to make (1) Unit 5.

6. Referring to Fusible Appliqué Basics (page 24), make the templates for the Daisy Block as listed in the Cutting Requirements.

7. Refer to the Large Daisy Block diagram to arrange the pieces onto Unit 5. Finish the raw edges of each shape with a decorative stitch. This completes the 12½" x 12½" (31.8 x 31.8cm) Large Daisy Block.
Optional: Add decorative stitching (see photo on page 42).

There are four layers total: Unit 5, Background Circle, Daisy, and Flower Center.

Quilting, Sewing & Appliqué: Essential Techniques for Beginners

Create Block

The Create Block teaches you how to embellish the block with thread. You will use thread and stitching to create definition to the spool on the block. This is another great way to add a personal touch.

FABRIC REQUIREMENTS:

Print—White Swirls (A)	⅜ yard (34.3cm)
Solid—Flame Red (B)	⅛ yard (11.4cm)
Print—Lime Weave (C)	⅛ yard (11.4cm)
Solid—Lemon (D)	⅛ yard (11.4cm)
Solid—Cherry Red (E)	⅛ yard (11.4cm)
Solid—Teal (F)	¼ yard (22.9cm)
Solid—Black (G)	⅛ yard (11.4cm)
Solid—Royal Blue (H)	⅛ yard (11.4cm)
Tonal—Iris (I)	⅛ yard (11.4cm)

SUPPLY REQUIREMENTS:

- Create templates (pages 115–116)
- Fusible web
- 50wt matching cotton threads
- Basic sewing supplies and tools
- Erasable marking pen

CUTTING REQUIREMENTS:

Print—White Swirls (Fabric A)
- (1) 10½" x 20½" (26.7 x 52.1cm) rectangle

Solid—Flame Red (Fabric B)
- (2) Spool Ends

Print—Lime Weave (Fabric C)
- (1) 2½" (6.4cm) x WOF strip. Subcut into:
  - (4) 2½" x 2½" (6.4 x 6.4cm) squares
- (2) Corner Circles

Solid—Lemon (Fabric D)
- (2) 1½" (3.8cm) x WOF strips
- (2) Splash #3

Solid—Cherry Red (Fabric E)
- (2) 1½" (3.8cm) x WOF strips
- (2) Splash #1

Solid—Teal (Fabric F)
- (2) Splash #2
- (1) set of Letters
- (1) Spool

Solid—Black (Fabric G)
- (1) Spool Hole

Solid—Royal Blue (Fabric H)
- (2) Corner Swirls

Tonal—Iris (Fabric I)
- (4) Cornerstone Circles

Watch a video tutorial on this block (and a bonus project).

Create Block 45

INSTRUCTIONS

1. Referring to Fusible Appliqué Basics (page 24), make the templates for the Create Block as listed in the Cutting Requirements.

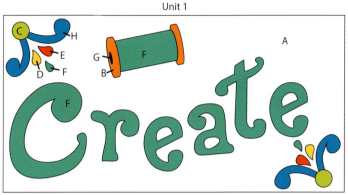
Unit 1

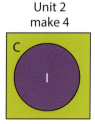
Unit 2
make 4

2. Arrange the appliqué pieces on the 10½" x 20½" (26.7 x 52.1cm) Fabric A rectangle. Press with the shiny side down. Finish the raw edges of each shape with a decorative stitch. This makes (1) Unit 1.

4. Center and press (1) Fabric I Cornerstone Circle onto (1) 2½" x 2½" (6.4 x 6.4cm) Fabric C square. Finish the raw edge of the shape with a decorative stitch, such as a blanket or satin stitch, to make (1) Unit 2. Repeat to make (4) Unit 2 squares total.

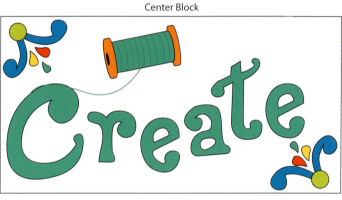
Center Block

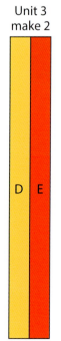
Unit 3
make 2

3. Draw lines on the spool and one line connecting the spool to the letter C using a water-soluble marking tool. Embroider directly over the drawn lines by machine or hand, creating the effect of thread on the spool. This completes the Center Block.

5. Sew (1) 1½" (3.8cm) x WOF Fabric D strip to the left side of (1) 1½" (3.8cm) x WOF Fabric E strip. This makes (1) Unit 3. Repeat to make a second Unit 3.

46 Quilting, Sewing & Appliqué: Essential Techniques for Beginners

Unit 4
cut 30

6. Cut (1) 2½" x 2½" (6.4 x 6.4cm) square from Unit 3. This makes (1) Unit 4. Repeat to make (30) Unit 4 squares total.

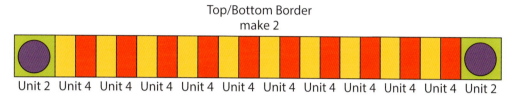

7. Sew together (10) Unit 4 squares, alternating the colors. Sew (1) Unit 2 to each end of the unit to make the Top Border. Repeat to make the Bottom Border.

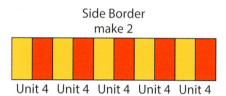

8. Sew together (5) Unit 4 squares to make (1) Side Border. Repeat to make a second Side Border.

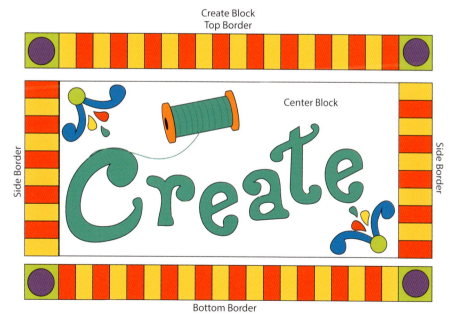

9. Sew (1) Side Border to each side of the Center Block. Sew the Top Border and Bottom Border to the top and to the bottom of the Center Block. This completes the 24½" x 14½" (62.2 x 36.8cm) Create Block.

Watch a video tutorial on this block (and a bonus project).

Smile Block

The Smile Block is an excellent project for practicing edge stitching on fusible appliqué using contrasting threads. This simple block is a perfect canvas for experimenting with different colors and weights of threads to embellish the letters and hearts.

FABRIC REQUIREMENTS:

Solid—Light Gray (A)
⅝ yard (57.2cm)

Solid—Sangria Red (B)
Fat Quarter

Tonal—Hot Pink (C)
⅛ yard (11.4cm)

Solid—Crimson Red (D)
¼ yard (22.9cm)

Solid—Wine Red (E)
¼ yard (22.9cm)

SUPPLY REQUIREMENTS:

- Smile templates (pages 117–118)
- Fusible web
- 50wt matching cotton threads
- Basic sewing supplies and tools

CUTTING REQUIREMENTS:

Solid—Light Gray (Fabric A)
- (1) 12½" x 20½" (31.8 x 52.1cm) rectangle
- (3) 2½" (6.4cm) x WOF strips. Subcut into:
  - (36) 2½" x 2½" (6.4 x 6.4cm) squares

Solid—Sangria Red (Fabric B)
- (1) X-Large Heart
- (2) Medium Hearts
- (1) X-Small Heart
- (1) set of Letters

Tonal—Hot Pink (Fabric C)
- (1) Large Heart
- (1) Medium Heart
- (2) Small Hearts
- (1) X-Small Heart

Solid—Crimson Red (Fabric D)
- (1) 2½" (6.4cm) x WOF strip. Subcut into:
  - (6) 2½" x 4½" (6.4 x 11.4cm) rectangles
- (1) X-Large Heart
- (1) Large Heart
- (2) Medium Hearts

Solid—Wine Red (Fabric E)
- (2) 2½" (6.4cm) x WOF strips. Subcut into:
  - (10) 2½" x 4½" (6.4 x 11.4cm) rectangles

Quilting, Sewing & Appliqué: Essential Techniques for Beginners

INSTRUCTIONS

1. Referring to Fusible Appliqué Basics (page 24), make the templates for the Smile Block onto the paper side of the fusible web.

Unit 1

2. Arrange the Letter pieces on the 12½" x 20½" (31.8 x 52.1cm) Fabric A rectangle. Press with the shiny side down. Finish the raw edges of each shape with a decorative stitch. This completes Unit 1.

   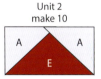

Unit 2 make 10

3. Place (1) 2½" x 2½" (6.4 x 6.4cm) Fabric A square on top of (1) 2½" x 4½" (6.4 x 11.4cm) Fabric E rectangle, right sides together. Align the left edges. Sew across the diagonal of the Fabric A square. Trim seam allowance to ¼" (6.4mm). Press the unit. Repeat on the opposite side with (1) 2½" x 2½" (6.4 x 6.4cm) Fabric A square. This makes (1) Unit 2. Repeat to make (10) Unit 2 rectangles total.

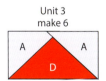
Unit 3 make 6

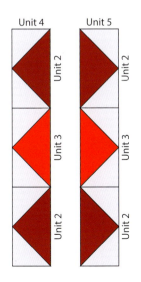
Unit 4 Unit 5

5. Sew (1) Unit 2 to each side of (1) Unit 3. This makes (1) Unit 4. Repeat to make (1) Unit 5.

4. Repeat step 3 with (12) 2½" x 2½" (6.4 x 6.4cm) Fabric A squares and (6) 2½" x 4½" (6.4 x 11.4cm) Fabric D rectangles. This makes (6) Unit 3 rectangles.

Smile Block

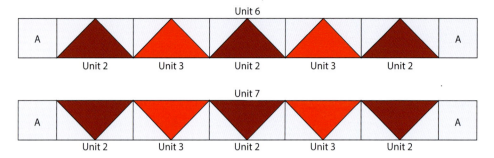

6. Sew together (3) Unit 2 rectangles and (2) Unit 3 rectangles, alternating them from left to right. Sew (1) 2½" x 2½" (6.4 x 6.4cm) Fabric A square to each end of the unit. This makes (1) Unit 6. Repeat to make (1) Unit 7.

7. Sew Unit 4 to the left side of Unit 1. Sew Unit 5 to the right side of Unit 1. Sew Unit 6 to the top of Unit 1. Sew Unit 7 to the bottom of Unit 1. This completes the 24½" x 16½" (62.2 x 41.9cm) Smile Block.

Watch a video tutorial on this block and its project.

Dream Block

We will explore a variation of the Flying Geese Block to create a lovely diagonal border on the Dream Block. It's always fun to play around with how traditional blocks are built to create a new look. This project also incorporates raw-edge appliqué around the stars and moon.

FABRIC REQUIREMENTS:

Tonal—Raspberry (A)
 ⅓ yard (30.5cm)
Print—White Swirls (B)
 ⅛ yard (11.4cm)
Solid—Pale Yellow (C)
 ⅛ yard (11.4cm)
Tonal—Deep Purple (D)
 Fat Quarter
Tonal—Buttercup (E)
 ⅛ yard (11.4cm)
Tonal—Powder Blue (F)
 ⅓ yard (30.5cm)
Solid—Cream (G)
 Fat Eighth

SUPPLY REQUIREMENTS:
- Dream templates (pages 119–120)
- Fusible web
- 50wt matching cotton threads
- Basic sewing supplies and tools

CUTTING REQUIREMENTS:

Tonal—Raspberry (Fabric A)
- (1) 2⅞" (7.3cm) x WOF strip. Subcut into:
  - (2) 2⅞" x 2⅞" (7.3 x 7.3cm) squares
- (2) 2½" (6.4cm) x WOF strips. Subcut into:
  - (8) 2½" x 4½" (6.4 x 11.4cm) rectangles
  - (16) 2½" x 2½" (6.4 x 6.4cm) squares

Print—White Swirls (Fabric B)
- (1) set of Letters

Solid—Pale Yellow (Fabric C)
- (1) X-Small Star
- (1) Small Star
- (1) Medium Star

Tonal—Deep Purple (Fabric D)
- (1) 16½" x 16½" (41.9 x 41.9cm) square

Tonal—Buttercup (Fabric E)
- (1) Small Star
- (1) Large Star

Tonal—Powder Blue (Fabric F)
- (1) 2⅞" (7.3cm) x WOF strip. Subcut into:
  - (2) 2⅞" x 2⅞" (7.3 x 7.3cm) squares
- (2) 2½" (6.4cm) x WOF strips. Subcut into:
  - (8) 2½" x 4½" (6.4 x 11.4cm) rectangles
  - (16) 2½" x 2½" (6.4 x 6.4cm) squares

Solid—Cream (Fabric G)
- (1) Moon

Dream Block 51

INSTRUCTIONS

1. Referring to Fusible Appliqué Basics (page 24), make the templates for the Dream Block as listed in the Cutting Requirements.

Center Block

2. Arrange the pieces on the 16½" x 16½" (41.9 x 41.9cm) Fabric D square. Press with the shiny side down. Machine stitch the raw edges of the letters with a decorative stitch. For moon and stars, straight stitch ⅛" (3.2mm) from the raw edge with contrasting thread for a raw-edge finish. This completes the Center Block.

> **Tip:** In this project, it is very important to keep the units separated by number. Consider using a water-soluble marker to label them on the wrong sides.

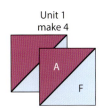

Unit 1 make 4

3. Referring to Half-Square Triangle Basics (page 21), pair (1) 2⅞" x 2⅞" (7.3 x 7.3cm) Fabric F square with (1) 2⅞" x 2⅞" (7.3 x 7.3cm) Fabric A square. Trim to 2½" x 2½" (6.4 x 6.4cm) to make (2) Unit 1 squares. Repeat to make (4) Unit 1 squares total.

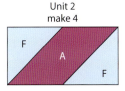

Unit 2 make 4

4. Place (1) 2½" x 2½" (6.4 x 6.4cm) Fabric F square on the left side of (1) 2½" x 4½" (6.4 x 11.4cm) Fabric A rectangle, right sides together. Sew across the diagonal of the Fabric F square from the upper center to the lower-left corner. Trim seam allowance to ¼" (6.4mm). Press. Repeat on the opposite side with (1) 2½" x 2½" (6.4 x 6.4cm) Fabric F. This completes (1) Unit 2. Repeat to make (4) Unit 2 rectangles total.

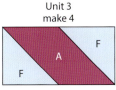

Unit 3 make 4

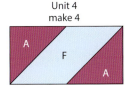

Unit 4 make 4

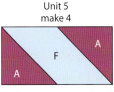

Unit 5 make 4

5. Repeat step 4 to make (4) Unit 3 rectangles. **Note:** The squares are sewn from the upper-left to the lower-right corner.

6. Repeat step 4 with (8) 2½" x 2½" (6.4 x 6.4cm) Fabric A squares and (4) 2½" x 4½" (6.4 x 11.4cm) Fabric F rectangles to make (4) Unit 4 rectangles.

7. Repeat step 4 with (8) 2½" x 2½" (6.4 x 6.4cm) Fabric A squares and (4) 2½" x 4½" (6.4 x 11.4cm) Fabric F rectangles to make (4) Unit 5 rectangles. **Note:** The squares are sewn from the upper-left to the lower-right corner.

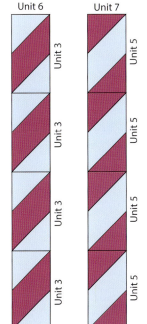

8. Arrange (4) Unit 3 rectangles end-to-end, and sew together to make (1) Unit 6. Arrange (4) Unit 5 rectangles end-to-end, and sew together to make (1) Unit 7.

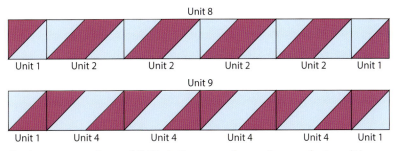

9. Arrange and sew (4) Unit 2 rectangles end-to-end. Sew (1) Unit 1 square to each end to make (1) Unit 8. Repeat with (4) Unit 4 rectangles to make (1) Unit 9.

Dream Block

Dream Block

10. Sew Unit 6 to the left side of the Center Block. Sew Unit 7 to the right side of the Center Block. Press seam allowances away from center. Sew Unit 8 to the top of the Center Block. Sew Unit 9 to the bottom of the Center Block. This completes the 20½" x 20½" (52.1 x 52.1cm) Dream Block.

54 Quilting, Sewing & Appliqué: Essential Techniques for Beginners

Hearts Block

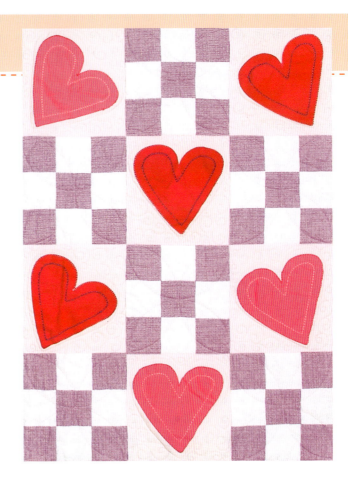

The Heart Block is a fun and easy design that makes for a great project to review the process of creating shapes with fusible appliqué and Checkerboard Blocks using strip piecing. This block is big enough that it can be quilted and bound to create a lovely mini quilt on its own.

FABRIC REQUIREMENTS:

Print—White Swirls (A)   ¼ yard (22.9cm)
Tonal—Hot Pink (B)   ¼ yard (22.9cm)
Solid—Bright Pink (C)   ¼ yard (22.9cm)
Solid—Powder Pink (D)   ¼ yard (22.9cm)
Print—Light Purple Weave (E)   ¼ yard (22.9cm)

SUPPLY REQUIREMENTS:

- Hearts template (page 121)
- Fusible web
- 50wt matching cotton threads
- Basic sewing supplies and tools

CUTTING REQUIREMENTS:

Print—White Swirls (Fabric A)
- (3) 2½" (6.4cm) x WOF strips

Tonal—Hot Pink (Fabric B)
- (3) Hearts

Solid—Bright Pink (Fabric C)
- (3) Hearts

Solid—Powder Pink (Fabric D)
- (1) 6½" (16.5cm) x WOF rectangle. Subcut into:
    - (6) 6½" x 6½" (16.5 x 16.5cm) squares

Print—Light Purple Weave (Fabric E)
- (3) 2½" (6.4cm) x WOF strips

Watch a video tutorial on this block (and a bonus project).

INSTRUCTIONS

1. Referring to Fusible Appliqué Basics (page 24), make the templates for the Hearts Block as listed in the Cutting Requirements.

Unit 1

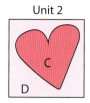
Unit 2

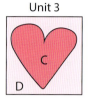
Unit 3

Unit 4

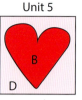
Unit 5

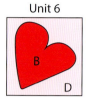
Unit 6

2. Arrange (1) Fabric C Heart on (1) 6½" x 6½" (16.5 x 16.5cm) Fabric D square. Press with the shiny side down. Use a straight stitch ⅛" (3.2mm) from the raw edge with contrasting thread for a raw-edge finish. This completes Unit 1.

3. Repeat step 2 with (2) Fabric C Hearts, (3) Fabric B Hearts, and (5) 6½" x 6½" (16.5 x 16.5cm) Fabric D squares to make Units 2 through 6.

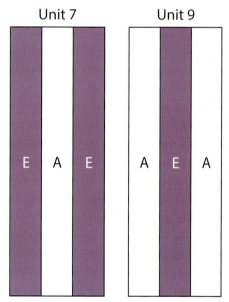

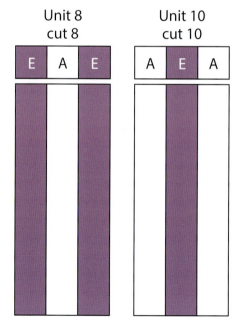

4. Sew (1) 2½" (6.4cm) x WOF Fabric E strip to each side of (1) 2½" (6.4cm) x WOF Fabric A strip to make (1) Unit 7. Repeat with (1) 2½" (6.4cm) x WOF Fabric A strip to each side of (1) 2½" (6.4cm) x WOF Fabric E strip to make (1) Unit 9.

5. From Unit 7, cut (8) 2½" x 6½" (6.4 x 16.5cm) strips to make Unit 8. From Unit 9, cut (10) 2½" x 6½" (6.4 x 16.5cm) strips to make Unit 10.

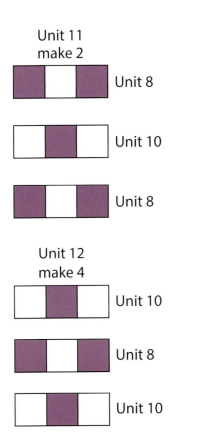

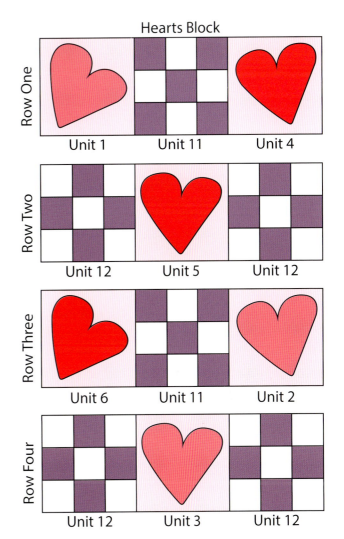

6. Sew (1) Unit 8 each to the top and bottom of (1) Unit 10 to complete (1) 6½" x 6½" (16.5 x 16.5cm) Unit 11. Repeat to make a second Unit 11. Repeat to make Unit 12, using (2) Unit 10 strips and (1) Unit 8, reversing placement. Repeat to make (4) Unit 12 squares total.

7. Sew together (1) Unit 1, (1) Unit 11, and (1) Unit 4, in that order from left to right, to make Row One. Refer to the Hearts Block diagram to make Rows Two through Four.

8. Sew together the (4) Rows in numerical order from top to bottom. This completes the 18½" x 24½" (47 x 62.2cm) Hearts Block.

Hearts Block

Starburst Block

The Starburst Block utilizes a variation of the Triangle-in-a-Square Unit found in the Laugh Block (page 35). We will make the units using paper templates and then add a small triangle in each corner. This unit is ideal for creating a block that resembles a star. You will need to make this block twice for the Inspire Quilt (page 87).

FABRIC REQUIREMENTS:

Solid—Light Blue (A)	¼ yard (22.9cm)
Solid—Dark Yellow (B)	Fat Eighth
Solid—Bright Blue (C)	¼ yard (22.9cm)
Print—White Swirls (D)	¼ yard (22.9cm)
Solid—Pale Yellow (E)	¼ yard (22.9cm)

SUPPLY REQUIREMENTS:

- Starburst templates (pages 122–123)
- Fusible web
- 50wt matching cotton threads
- Basic sewing supplies and tools
- *Optional:* Creative Grids 2 Peaks in 1 Triangle Quilt Ruler

CUTTING REQUIREMENTS:

Solid—Light Blue (Fabric A)
- (1) 4½" (11.4cm) x WOF rectangle. Subcut into:
  - (4) Template 2 (T6-2)

Solid—Dark Yellow (Fabric B)
- (1) Large Star
- (4) Medium Stars

Solid—Bright Blue (Fabric C)
- (1) 4½" (11.4cm) x WOF rectangles. Subcut into:
  - (5) 4½" x 4½" (11.4 x 11.4cm) squares

Print—White Swirls (Fabric D)
- (1) 4½" (11.4cm) x WOF rectangle. Subcut into:
  - (4) Template 1 (T6-1)
  - (4) Template 3 (T6-3)

Solid—Pale Yellow (Fabric E)
- (1) 2½" (6.4cm) x WOF strip. Subcut into:
  - (8) 2½" x 2½" (6.4 x 6.4cm) squares
- (4) Small Stars

Watch a video tutorial on this block and its project.

58 Quilting, Sewing & Appliqué: Essential Techniques for Beginners

INSTRUCTIONS

1. Referring to Fusible Appliqué Basics (page 24), make the templates for the Starburst Block as listed in the Cutting Requirements.

Unit 1
make 4

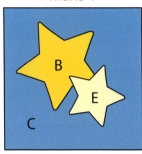

Unit 2
make 1

2. Refer to Unit 1 diagram to arrange (1) Fabric B Medium Star and (1) Fabric E Small Star on (1) 4½" x 4½" (11.4 x 11.4cm) Fabric C square. Press with the shiny side down. This makes (1) Unit 1. Repeat to make (4) Unit 1 squares total.

3. Refer to Unit 2 diagram to arrange (1) Fabric B Large Star on (1) 4½" x 4½" (11.4 x 11.4cm) Fabric C square. Press with the shiny side down. This makes (1) Unit 2.

4. Finish the raw edges of each shape with a decorative stitch, such as a blanket or satin stitch. Use matching threads. This completes (4) Unit 1 squares and (1) Unit 2.

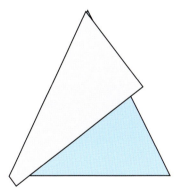
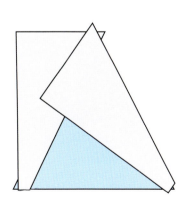
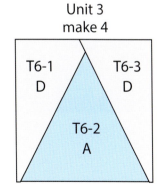

Unit 3
make 4

5. Place (1) Fabric D Template 1 on top of (1) Fabric A Template 2 right sides together. Align the left edges. Sew the triangles together along the left side. Press the T6-1 triangle open. Repeat on the right side using (1) Fabric D Template 3 triangle. Trim the unit to measure 4½" x 4½" (11.4 x 11.4cm). Repeat to make (4) Unit 3 squares total.

Starburst Block

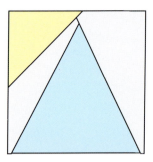 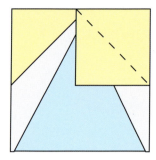 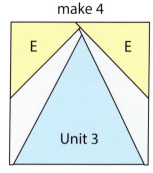

Unit 4 make 4

6. Place (1) 2½" x 2½" (6.4 x 6.4cm) Fabric E square on the top-left corner of (1) Unit 3, right sides together. Sew across the diagonal. Trim seam allowance to ¼" (6.4mm). Press. Repeat the opposite side with (1) 2½" x 2½" (6.4 x 6.4cm) Fabric E square. This makes (1) Unit 4. Make (4) Unit 4 squares total.

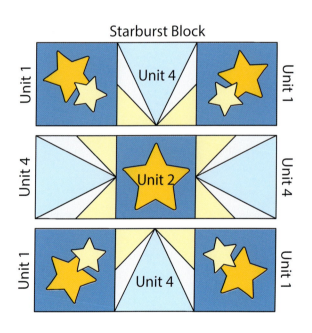

Starburst Block

7. Sew (1) Unit 1 to each side of (1) Unit 4 to make the top row. Repeat to make the bottom row. Sew (1) Unit 4 to each side of (1) Unit 2 to make the middle row. Pay attention to the orientation of each unit. Sew together the rows to make (1) 12½" x 12½" (31.8 x 31.8cm) Starburst Block.

Tip: Use thread to embellish the block with decorative stitches and swirl vine details.

Stars Block

We will learn how to create the Stars Block with strip piecing. This is also a great block to learn how to evenly space and sew the fusible appliqué shapes across the pieced background.

FABRIC REQUIREMENTS:

Solid—Dark Yellow (A)   Fat Eighth
Solid—Pale Yellow (B)   ⅛ yard (11.4cm)
Solid—Bright Green (C)   ⅛ yard (11.4cm)
Solid—Green Apple (D)   ⅛ yard (11.4cm)

SUPPLY REQUIREMENTS:

- Stars templates (page 124)
- Fusible web
- 50wt matching cotton threads
- Basic sewing supplies and tools

CUTTING REQUIREMENTS:

Solid—Dark Yellow (Fabric A)
- (3) Large Stars
- (2) Small Stars

Solid—Pale Yellow (Fabric B)
- (3) Medium Stars

Solid—Bright Green (Fabric C)
- (2) 2½" (6.4cm) x WOF strips

Solid—Green Apple (Fabric D)
- (2) 2½" (6.4cm) x WOF strips

Watch a video tutorial on the next two blocks, one project, and a bonus project.

INSTRUCTIONS

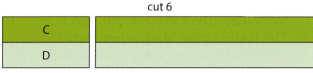

1. Sew (1) 2½" (6.4cm) x WOF Fabric C strip to the top of (1) 2½" (6.4cm) x WOF Fabric D strip to make (1) Unit 1. Repeat to make a second Unit 1.

2. Cut (1) 4½" x 7½" (11.4 x 19.1cm) rectangle from Unit 1. This makes (1) Unit 2. Repeat to make (6) Unit 2 rectangles total.

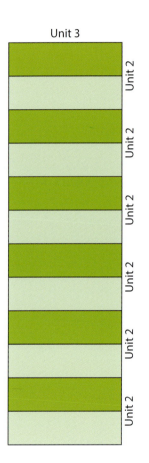

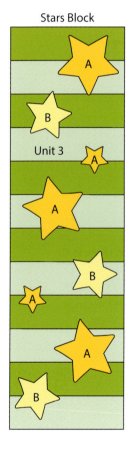

3. Sew together (6) Unit 2 rectangles to make (1) 7½" x 24½" (19.1 x 62.2cm) Unit 3.

4. Referring to Fusible Appliqué Basics (page 24), make the templates for the Stars Block as listed in the Cutting Requirements.

5. Refer to the Stars Block diagram to arrange the pieces on Unit 3. Press with the shiny side down. Finish the raw edges of each star with a decorative stitch. This completes the 7½" x 24½" (19.1 x 62.2cm) Stars Block.

Mini Daisies Block

The Mini Daisies Block is a delightful and straightforward project. You will gain knowledge about layering different pieces for fusible appliqué onto a background. These blocks are perfect for honing your edge stitching skills around each shape.

FABRIC REQUIREMENTS:

Print—White Floral (A)   Fat Eighth
Solid—Bright Orange (B)   Fat Eighth
Tonal—Violet (C)   ⅛ yard (11.4cm)
Print—Lime Weave (D)   ¼ yard (22.9cm)

SUPPLY REQUIREMENTS:
- Mini Daisies templates (page 124)
- Fusible web
- 50wt matching cotton threads
- Basic sewing supplies and tools

CUTTING REQUIREMENTS:

Print—White Floral (Fabric A)
- (5) Daisies

Solid—Bright Orange (Fabric B)
- (5) Daisy Centers

Tonal—Violet (Fabric C)
- (5) Daisy Backgrounds

Print—Lime Weave (Fabric D)
- (5) 4½" x 4½" (11.4 x 11.4cm) squares

See page 61 for a QR code for this project.

Mini Daisies Block

INSTRUCTIONS

1. Referring to Fusible Appliqué Basics (page 24), make the templates for the Mini Daisies Block on the paper side of the fusible web. Make as many as listed in the Cutting Requirements.

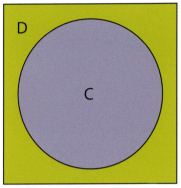
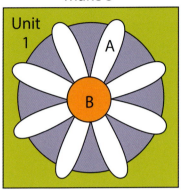

2. Arrange (1) Fabric C Daisy Background onto (1) 4½" x 4½" (11.4 x 11.4cm) Fabric D square. Press with the shiny side down. This makes (1) Unit 1. Repeat to make (5) Unit 1 squares total.

3. Arrange and press (1) Fabric A Daisy onto (1) Unit 1. Arrange and press (1) Fabric B Daisy Center onto the unit. This makes (1) Unit 2. Repeat to make (5) Unit 2 squares total.

4. Finish the raw edges of each shape with a decorative stitch, such as a blanket or satin stitch. Use matching threads. This completes the (5) Unit 2 squares.

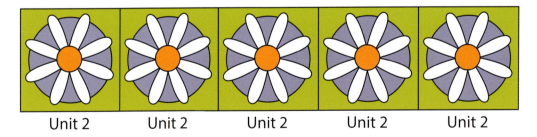

5. Sew together the (5) Unit 2 squares. This completes the 4½" x 20½" (11.4 x 52.1cm) Mini Daisies Block.

Quilting, Sewing & Appliqué: Essential Techniques for Beginners

Making Pretty Projects

In this section, let's make some items for our creative journey using some of the block designs and techniques you've learned. You'll pick up a few more skills here, such as how to sew in a zipper and work with clear vinyl. Gift these to your friends; we promise, they'll be impressed by your mad skills!

Imagine Bench Pillow

The Imagine Bench Pillow is an excellent project for featuring the Imagine Block. This project will guide you through sewing strips of fabric together and then cutting them to create a checkerboard border, showcasing a fast-and-easy technique for making any checkerboard block.

FABRIC REQUIREMENTS:

Solid—Light Blue (A)	½ yard (45.7cm)
Solid—Hot Pink (B)	Fat Quarter
Print—White Floral (C)	Fat Eighth
Solid—Bright Orange (D)	Fat Eighth
Solid—Dark Yellow (E)	⅓ yard (30.5cm)
Tonal—Raspberry (F)	1¼ yards (114.3cm)

SUPPLY REQUIREMENTS:

- Imagine templates (pages 102–104)
- Fusible web
- Stuffing
- 50wt matching cotton threads
- Basic sewing supplies and tools

CUTTING REQUIREMENTS:

Solid—Light Blue (Fabric A)
- (1) 12½" x 40½" (31.8 x 102.9cm) rectangle

Solid—Hot Pink (Fabric B)
- (1) set of Letters
- (1) "I" Dot

Print—White Floral (Fabric C)
- (2) Large Daisies
- (2) Small Daisies

Solid—Bright Orange (Fabric D)
- (2) Large Daisy Centers
- (2) Small Daisy Centers

Solid—Dark Yellow (Fabric E)
- (2) 2½" (6.4cm) x WOF strips

Tonal—Raspberry (Fabric F)
- (2) 2½" (6.4cm) x WOF strips
- (1) 16½" x 44½" (41.9 x 113cm) rectangle (piece as needed)

INSTRUCTIONS

1. Make (1) 12½" x 40½" (31.8 x 102.9cm) Imagine Block (page 28).

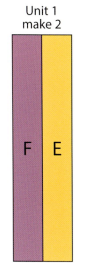

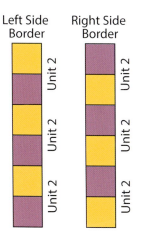

2. Sew (1) 2½" (6.4cm) x WOF Fabric F strip to the left side of (1) 2½" (6.4cm) x WOF Fabric E strip lengthwise to make (1) Unit 1. Repeat to make a second Unit 1.

3. Cut (1) 2½" x 4½" (6.4 x 11.4cm) rectangle from Unit 1 to create (1) Unit 2. Repeat to make (28) Unit 2 rectangles. Use a ruler to ensure the correct size of each.

4. Sew together (3) Unit 2 rectangles end-to-end in the order shown. This makes the Pillow Left Side Border. Repeat to make the Pillow Right Side Border.

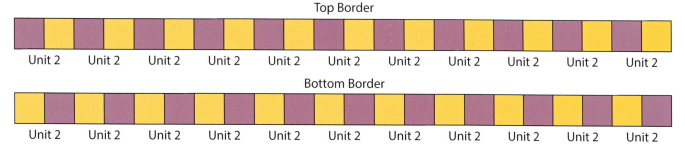

5. Sew together (11) Unit 2 rectangles end-to-end in the order shown. This makes the Pillow Top Border. Repeat to make the Pillow Bottom Border.

Imagine Bench Pillow

6. Lay out the Imagine Block, Pillow Left Side Border, Pillow Right Side Border, Pillow Top Border, and Pillow Bottom Border as shown. Rotate the borders to create a checkerboard pattern around the center.

7. Sew the Pillow Left Side Border to the left of the Imagine Block. Press the seam open. Repeat with the Pillow Right Side Border to the right of the block. Sew the Pillow Top Border and Pillow Bottom Border on the top and bottom respectively. This makes the 16½" x 44½" (41.9 x 113cm) Pillow Front.

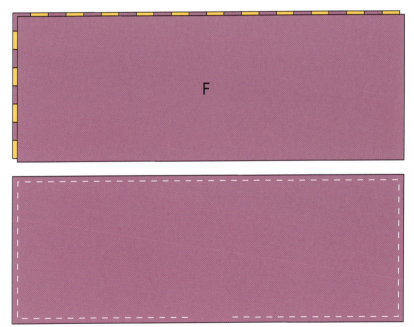

8. Place the 16½" x 44½" (41.9 x 113cm) Fabric F rectangle right sides together with the Pillow Front. Align the raw edges, pin, and stitch around, leaving a 3"–4" (7.6–10.2cm) opening for turning.

9. Turn the pillow right side out through the opening. Fold the opening's raw edges in by ¼" (6.4mm). Press around all the sides, including the opening.

10. Insert the stuffing. Hand stitch the opening closed with a ladder stitch to complete the pillow.

Sun Fabric Baskets

The Sun Fabric Basket is an enjoyable and straightforward project that uses any square block you choose. Learn how simple it is to transform a flat piece into a 3D object using box corners.

FABRIC REQUIREMENTS:

Print—Orange Weave (A)   ¼ yard (22.9cm)
Print—Yellow Weave (B)   ⅛ yard (11.4cm)
Solid—Pale Yellow (C)   ⅔ yard (61cm)
Solid—Light Teal (D)   ⅝ yard (57.2cm)

SUPPLY REQUIREMENTS:

- Sun templates (page 110)
- Fusible web
- 50wt matching cotton threads
- Basic sewing supplies and tools
- Erasable marking pen
- (2) 17½" x 17½" (44.5 x 44.5cm) pieces of fusible fleece
- (2) 17½" x 17½" (44.5 x 44.5cm) pieces of fusible stabilizer

CUTTING REQUIREMENTS:

Print—Orange Weave (Fabric A)
- (16) Fabric Basket Outer Rays

Print—Yellow Weave (Fabric B)
- (16) Fabric Basket Inner Rays

Solid—Pale Yellow (Fabric C)
- (2) Fabric Basket Sun Centers
- (2) 17½" x 17½" (44.5 x 44.5cm) squares

Solid—Light Teal (Fabric D)
- (2) 17½" x 17½" (44.5 x 44.5cm) squares

INSTRUCTIONS

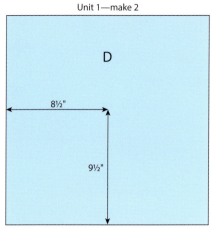

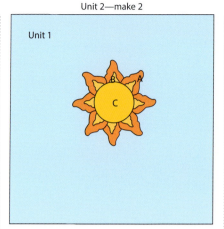

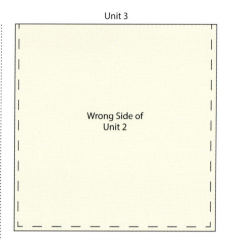

1. On one side of a 17½" x 17½" (44.5 x 44.5cm) Fabric D square, measure 8½" (21.6cm) in from one side. Measure 9½" (24.1cm) up from the bottom. Make a dot with an erasable marking pen where they meet in the middle, which represents the center position of the Sun appliqué. This makes (1) Unit 1. Repeat to make a second Unit 1.

2. Referring to Fusible Appliqué Basics (page 24), make the templates for the Sun Basket as listed in the Cutting Requirements.

3. Arrange the assorted Sun Basket pieces onto Unit 1, centering on the mark from step 1. Referring to steps 2 and 3 of Sun Block (page 34), press to make Unit 2. Repeat to make a second Unit 2. Use matching threads to finish the raw edges of each shape with a decorative stitch, such as a blanket or satin stitch.

4. Following the manufacturer's instructions, press (1) 17½" x 17½" (44.5 x 44.5cm) fusible fleece to the wrong side of each square to complete (2) Unit 2.

5. Place the (2) Unit 2/fusible fleece squares right sides together. Sew down each side and across the bottom to make Unit 3. Pay attention to top and bottom, as the sun is not perfectly centered on the base fabric.

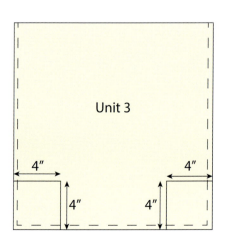

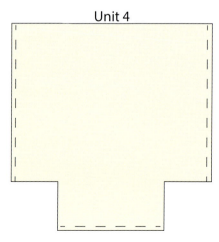

6. With a thin marker, draw a 4" x 4" (10.2 x 10.2cm) square on a bottom corner of Unit 3. Repeat on the opposite side of Unit 3. Cut out the squares to make Unit 4.

70 Quilting, Sewing & Appliqué: Essential Techniques for Beginners

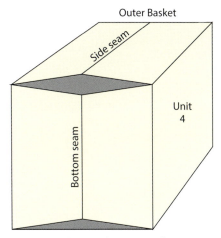
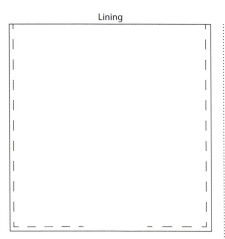
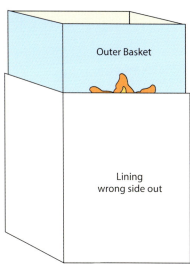

7. Open the cut bottom of Unit 4. Flatten the bottom edge so it aligns with one side edge, and sew the two edges together. Repeat with the other bottom edge and side, making the Outer Basket. Turn the Outer Basket right side out.

8. Following the manufacturer's instructions, press (1) 17½" x 17½" (44.5 x 44.5cm) fusible stabilizer to the wrong side of each 17½" x 17½" (44.5 x 44.5cm) Fabric C square.

9. Place the (2) Fabric C squares right sides together. Sew down each side and across the bottom, leaving a 4" (10.2cm) opening on the bottom for turning. This makes the Lining.

10. Repeat steps 6 and 7 with the Lining to create the basket bottom.

11. Slide the Lining over the Outer Basket with right sides together, aligning the side seams and top raw edges. Pin or clip together. Sew around the top edges to attach the Lining to the Outer Basket.

12. Turn the fabric basket right side out through the 4" (10.2cm) opening in the Lining from Step 9. Press. Topstitch the opening closed.

13. Push the Lining into the Outer Basket. Press the top edge to ensure the Lining stays flat inside the basket. Topstitch around the outer edge.

14. Fold the top of the basket down 1"–2" (2.5–5.1cm) or as desired to create a decorative element.

Sun Fabric Baskets

Alternative Sizes for Fabric Baskets

Note: You also need (2) pieces of fusible fleece and (2) pieces of fusible stabilizer in the same size as the cutting requirements.

Basket Size	Fabric Requirements	Cutting Requirements	Corner Measurement (step 6)
XXS: 5" (12.7cm)	Fabric C: Fat Quarter Fabric D: Fat Quarter	Fabric C: (2) 9" x 9" (22.9 x 22.9cm) squares Fabric D: (2) 9" x 9" (22.9 x 22.9cm) squares	2" x 2" (5.1 x 5.1cm)
XS: 6" (15.2cm)	Fabric C: ⅓ yard (30.5cm) Fabric D: ⅓ yard (30.5cm)	Fabric C: (2) 11" x 11" (27.9 x 27.9cm) squares Fabric D: (2) 11" x 11" (27.9 x 27.9cm) squares	2½" x 2½" (6.4 x 6.4cm)
Small: 7" (17.8cm)	Fabric C: ½ yard (45.7cm) Fabric D: ½ yard (45.7cm)	Fabric C: (2) 13" x 13" (33 x 33cm) squares Fabric D: (2) 13" x 13" (33 x 33cm) squares	3" x 3" (7.6 x 7.6cm)
Medium: 8" (20.3cm)	Fabric C: ½ yard (45.7cm) Fabric D: ½ yard (45.7cm)	Fabric C: (2) 15" x 15" (38.1 x 38.1cm) squares Fabric D: (2) 15" x 15" (38.1 x 38.1cm) squares	3½" x 3½" (8.9 x 8.9cm)
Large: 9" (22.9cm)	Fabric C: ⅝ yard (57.2cm) Fabric D: ⅝ yard (57.2cm)	Fabric C: (2) 17" x 17" (43.2 x 43.2cm) squares Fabric D: (2) 17" x 17" (43.2 x 43.2cm) squares	4" x 4" (10.2 x 10.2cm)
XL: 11" (27.9cm)	Fabric C: ⅔ yard (61cm) Fabric D: ⅔ yard (61cm)	Fabric C: (2) 21" x 21" (53.3 x 53.3cm) squares Fabric D: (2) 21" x 21" (53.3 x 53.3cm) squares	5" x. 5" (12.7 x 12.7cm)
Rectangle: 4½" x 7" x 7" (11.4 x 17.8 x 17.8cm)	Fabric C: Fat Quarter Fabric D: Fat Quarter	Fabric C: (2) 7½" x 10" (19.1 x 25.4cm) rectangles Fabric D: (2) 7½" x 10" (19.1 x 25.4cm) rectangles	1½" x 1½" (3.8 x 3.8cm)

Laugh Table Runner

The Laugh Table Runner will teach you how to create Flying Geese Blocks. These blocks feature triangles made from squares and rectangles of fabric, using an easy technique to achieve a complex look.

FABRIC REQUIREMENTS:

Print—White Floral (A)	¼ yard (22.9cm)
Solid—Bright Orange (B)	¼ yard (22.9cm)
Solid—Pale Yellow (C)	⅓ yard (30.5cm)
Solid—Flame Red (D)	½ yard (45.7cm)
Print—Orange Weave (E)	½ yard (45.7cm)
Solid—Peach (F)	⅓ yard (30.5cm)
Quilt Back	1¼ yards (114.3cm)

SUPPLY REQUIREMENTS:

- Laugh templates (pages 110–112)
- Fusible web
- 50wt matching cotton threads
- Basic sewing supplies and tools
- 20" x 44" (50.8 x 111.8cm) rectangle of batting

CUTTING REQUIREMENTS:

Print—White Floral (Fabric A)
- (2) Large Daisies
- (2) Small Daisies

Solid—Bright Orange (Fabric B)
- (1) 2⅞" (7.3cm) x WOF strip. Subcut into:
  - (10) 2⅞" x 2⅞" (7.3 x 7.3cm) squares

Solid—Pale Yellow (Fabric C)
- (1) 1½" (3.8cm) x WOF strip. Subcut into:
  - (16) 1½" x 1½" (3.8 x 3.8cm) squares
- (2) 2⅞" (7.3cm) x WOF strips. Subcut into:
  - (20) 2⅞" x 2⅞" (7.3 x 7.3cm) squares

Solid—Flame Red (Fabric D)
- (1) 2½" (6.4cm) x WOF strip. Subcut into:
  - (4) 2½" x 2½" (6.4 x 6.4cm) squares
- (3) 2½" (6.4cm) x WOF strips
- (1) set of Letters

Print—Orange Weave (Fabric E)
- (1) 2⅞" (7.3cm) x WOF strip. Subcut into:
  - (10) 2⅞" x 2⅞" (7.3 x 7.3cm) squares
- (2) Large Daisy Centers
- (2) Small Daisy Centers

Solid—Peach (Fabric F)
- (1) 8½" (21.6cm) x WOF rectangle. Subcut into:
  - (1) 8½" x 32½" (21.6 x 82.6cm) rectangle

Quilt Back Fabric
- (1) 20" x 44" (50.8 x 111.8cm) rectangle

INSTRUCTIONS

1. Referring to Fusible Appliqué Basics (page 24), make the templates for the Laugh Runner as listed in the Cutting Requirements.

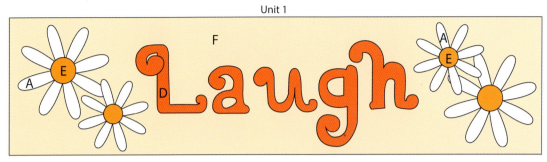
Unit 1

2. Refer to Unit 1 diagram to arrange the pieces onto the 8½" x 32½" (21.6 x 82.6cm) Fabric F rectangle. Press with the shiny side down. Finish the raw edges of each shape with a decorative stitch. This completes Unit 1.

3. Place (1) 1½" x 1½" (3.8 x 3.8cm) Fabric C square on the top-left corner of (1) 2½" x 2½" (6.4 x 6.4cm) Fabric D square, right sides together. Sew across the diagonal of the Fabric C square. Trim seam allowance to ¼" (6.4mm) and press.

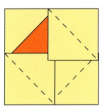
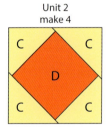
Unit 2
make 4

4. Rotate the unit 90 degrees counterclockwise, and follow step 3 until Fabric C squares are added to the remaining corners of the Fabric D square. This makes (1) Unit 2. Repeat to make (4) Unit 2 squares total.

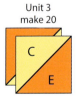
Unit 3
make 20

Unit 4
make 20

5. Referring to Half-Square Triangle Basics (page 21), pair (10) 2⅞" x 2⅞" (7.3 x 7.3cm) Fabric C squares with (10) 2⅞" x 2⅞" (7.3 x 7.3cm) Fabric E squares to make (20) Unit 3 squares. Pair (10) 2⅞" x 2⅞" (7.3 x 7.3cm) Fabric C squares and (10) 2⅞" x 2⅞" (7.3 x 7.3cm) Fabric B squares to make (20) Unit 4 squares. Trim to 2½" x 2½" (6.4 x 6.4cm).

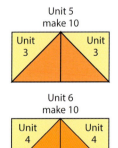
Unit 5
make 10

Unit 6
make 10

6. Arrange (2) Unit 3 squares, and sew together to make (1) Unit 5. Repeat to make (10) 2½" x 4½" (6.4 x 11.4cm) Unit 5 rectangles total. Repeat with the Unit 4 squares to make (10) 2½" x 4½" (6.4 x 11.4cm) Unit 6 rectangles total.

Quilting, Sewing & Appliqué: Essential Techniques for Beginners

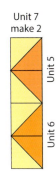

Unit 7
make 2

7. Arrange (1) Unit 5 and (1) Unit 6. Sew together to make (1) Unit 7. Repeat to make a second Unit 7.

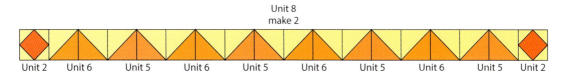

8. Arrange (2) Unit 2 squares, (4) Unit 5 rectangles, and (4) Unit 6 rectangles. Sew together to make (1) Unit 8. Repeat to make a second Unit 8.

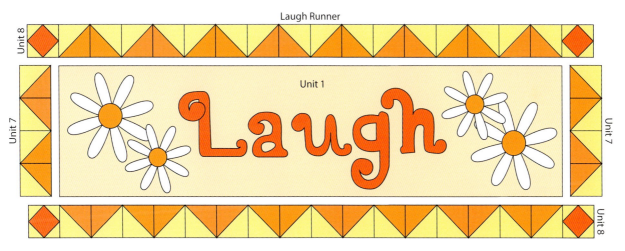

9. Sew (1) Unit 7 to each side of Unit 1. Sew (1) Unit 8 each to the top and bottom of Unit 1. This makes the 36½" x 12½" (92.7 x 31.8cm) Laugh Runner quilt top.

10. Layer the quilt top, batting, and quilt back (see page 94). Quilt as desired (see page 97).

11. Sew (3) 2½" (6.4cm) Fabric D strips together end-to-end with 45-degree seams to make the binding. Fold this long strip in half lengthwise with wrong sides together and press. Bind as desired (see page 98)

Laugh Table Runner

Dream Pocket Pillow

With the Dream Pocket Pillow, we will learn how to add a zipper and a pocket to a project. These skills are essential for creating bags, pillows, and clothes. Though sewing a zipper can sound intimidating, once you have made a project with a zipper, you will see how easy it can be.

FABRIC REQUIREMENTS:

Tonal—Raspberry (A)
⅓ yard (30.5cm)
Print—White Swirls (B)
⅛ yard (11.4cm)
Solid—Pale Yellow (C)
⅛ yard (11.4cm)
Tonal—Deep Purple (D)
Fat Quarter
Tonal—Buttercup (E)
⅛ yard (11.4cm)
Tonal—Powder Blue (F)
⅓ yard (30.5cm)
Solid—Cream (G)
¾ yard (68.6cm)

SUPPLY REQUIREMENTS:

- Dream templates (pages 119–120)
- Fusible web
- 50wt matching cotton threads
- Basic sewing supplies and tools
- 22" (55.9cm) zipper
- 20" x 20" (50.8 x 50.8cm) pillow form

CUTTING REQUIREMENTS:

Tonal—Raspberry (Fabric A)
- (1) 2⅞" (7.3cm) x WOF strip. Subcut into:
  - (2) 2⅞" x 2⅞" (7.3 x 7.3cm) squares
- (2) 2½" (6.4cm) x WOF strips. Subcut into:
  - (8) 2½" x 4½" (6.4 x 11.4cm) rectangles
  - (16) 2½" x 2½" (6.4 x 6.4cm) squares

Print—White Swirls (Fabric B)
- (1) set of Letters

Solid—Pale Yellow (Fabric C)
- (1) X-Small Star
- (1) Small Star
- (1) Medium Star

Tonal—Deep Purple (Fabric D)
- (1) 16½" x 16½" (41.9 x 41.9cm) square

Tonal—Buttercup (Fabric E)
- (1) Small Star
- (1) Large Star

Tonal—Powder Blue (Fabric F)
- (1) 2⅞" (7.3cm) x WOF strip. Subcut into:
  - (2) 2⅞" x 2⅞" (7.3 x 7.3cm) squares
- (2) 2½" (6.4cm) x WOF strips. Subcut into:
  - (8) 2½" x 4½" (6.4 x 11.4cm) rectangles
  - (16) 2½" x 2½" (6.4 x 6.4cm) squares

Solid—Cream (Fabric G)
- (1) 20½" (52.1cm) x WOF rectangle. Subcut into:
  - (2) 20½" x 20½" (52.1 x 52.1cm) squares
- (1) Moon

INSTRUCTIONS

1. Make (1) 20½" x 20½" (52.1 x 52.1cm) Dream Block (page 51).

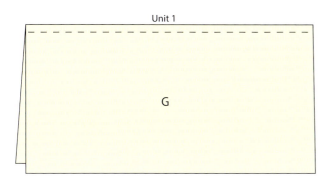

2. Fold (1) 20½" x 20½" (52.1 x 52.1cm) Fabric G square in half, wrong sides together. Topstitch across the fold to make (1) 10¼" x 20½" (26 x 52.1cm) Unit 1.

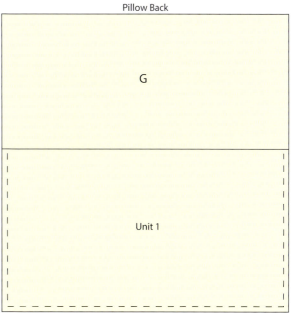

3. Place Unit 1 on top of (1) 20½" x 20½" (52.1 x 52.1cm) Fabric G square, aligning bottom edges. The sewn fold is the top of Unit 1. Baste ½" (1.3cm) from the edge, down the sides and across the bottom, to finish the Pillow Back.

Dream Pocket Pillow

4. Place the zipper right side up on a flat surface. Place the Pillow Front on top, right sides together, aligning the top edges and making sure the zipper pull will close ½" (1.3cm) from the side. Pin or clip the zipper in place. Use a zipper foot to sew zipper tape to pillow edge to make Unit 2.

5. Flip zipper up as shown and press. Topstitch the Pillow Front a scant ¼" (6.4mm) from fold as shown to make Unit 3.

Dream Pocket Pillow in Printed Fabric

This pattern can be reused with a variety of prints to make it your own.

FABRIC REQUIREMENTS:

Print—Turquoise Batik (A)	⅓ yard (30.5cm)
Tonal—Dark Turquoise (B)	⅛ yard (11.4cm)
Prints—Assorted Turquoise (C)	⅛ yard (11.4cm)
Print—Medium Turquoise Mini Geometric (D)	Fat Quarter
Prints—Assorted (E)	⅛ yard (11.4cm)
Tonal—Cream (F)	⅓ yard (30.5cm)
Print—Mini Star (G)	¾ yard (68.6cm)

78 Quilting, Sewing & Appliqué: Essential Techniques for Beginners

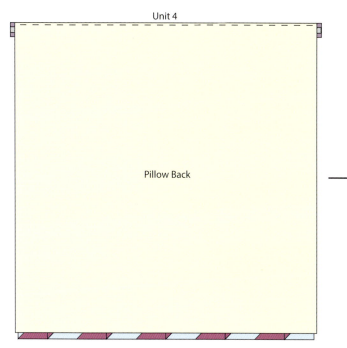

6. Place the Pillow Back on top of Unit 3, right sides together, aligning the Back's top edge with the zipper's remaining raw edge. Pin or clip the pieces together. Use a zipper foot to sew the pieces together to make Unit 4. Flip open and topstitch front side of zipper to make Unit 5 as you did for pillow front. Pull the zipper open to the middle and trim the zipper end even with the side of the pillow.

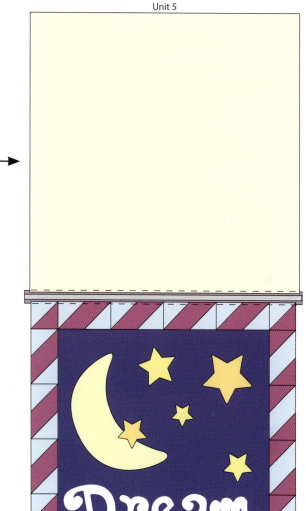

7. Align the Pillow Front and Pillow Back, right sides together, aligning the raw edges. Ensure the zipper is open, then sew down each side and across the bottom to complete the Pillowcase.

8. Turn the Pillowcase right side out through the zipper opening. Insert the pillow form and zip closed to complete the Dream Pocket Pillow.

Starburst Zipper Pouch

The Starburst Zipper Pouch gives us another chance to practice our zipper skills. You will also learn how to work with vinyl to create this fun, see-through bag.

FABRIC REQUIREMENTS:

Solid—Dark Yellow (A)	¼ yard (22.9cm)
Solid—Bright Blue (B)	⅔ yard (61cm)
Solid—Pale Yellow (C)	¼ yard (22.9cm)

SUPPLY REQUIREMENTS:
- Starburst templates (page 123)
- Fusible web
- 50wt matching cotton threads
- Basic sewing supplies and tools
- (2) 6½" x 10½" (16.5 x 26.7cm) pieces of clear vinyl
- Basic glue stick
- 12" (30.5cm) matching zipper
- Zipper foot

CUTTING REQUIREMENTS:

Solid—Dark Yellow (Fabric A)
- (1) 3" x 10" (7.6 x 25.4cm) rectangle
- (2) Large Stars
- (4) Medium Stars

Solid—Bright Blue (Fabric B)
- (2) 4½" (11.4cm) x WOF rectangles. Subcut into:
  - (6) 4½" x 4½" (11.4 x 11.4cm) squares
  - (2) 4½" x 12½" (11.4 x 31.8cm) rectangles
- (3) 2½" (6.4cm) x WOF strips. Subcut into:
  - (2) 2½" x 12½" (6.4 x 31.8cm) strips
  - (4) 2½" x 6½" (6.4 x 16.5cm) rectangles
  - (6) 2½" x 2½" (6.4 x 6.4cm) squares
  - (2) 1" x 2" (2.5 x 5.1cm) rectangles

Solid—Pale Yellow (Fabric C)
- (1) 2½" (6.4cm) x WOF strip. Subcut into:
  - (6) 2½" x 2½" (6.4 x 6.4cm) squares
- (4) Small Stars

Quilting, Sewing & Appliqué: Essential Techniques for Beginners

INSTRUCTIONS

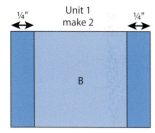

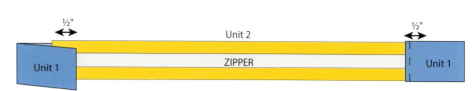

1. Fold in each short edge of (1) 1" x 2" (2.5 x 5.1cm) Fabric B rectangle by ¼" (6.4mm) and press to make (1) Unit 1. Repeat to make a second Unit 1. Fold each Unit 1 in half horizontally, wrong sides together, and press.

2. Slide (1) Unit 1 over one end of the zipper as shown, covering about ½" (1.3cm). Topstitch across Unit 1 and the zipper to hold them in place.

3. Slide (1) Unit 1 over the other end of the zipper, and clip in place. Measure the zipper and Unit 1. This unit needs to measure 12½" (31.8cm) long. Trim the zipper and/or move the second Unit 1 to reach the correct length. Topstitch second Unit 1 in place to make (1) Unit 2.

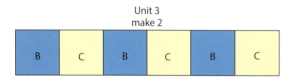

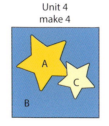

4. Sew together (3) 2½" x 2½" (6.4 x 6.4cm) Fabric B squares and (3) 2½" x 2½" (6.4 x 6.4cm) Fabric C squares, alternating them from left to right. This makes (1) 2½" x 12½" (6.4 x 31.8cm) Unit 3. Repeat to make a second Unit 3.

5. Referring to Fusible Appliqué Basics (page 24), make the templates for the Starburst Zipper Pouch as listed in the Cutting Requirements.

6. Arrange (1) Fabric A Medium Star and (1) Fabric C Small Star on (1) 4½" x 4½" (11.4 x 11.4cm) Fabric B square. Press with the shiny side down. This makes (1) Unit 4. Repeat to make (4) Unit 4 squares total.

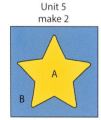

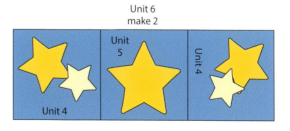

7. Arrange (1) Fabric A Large Star on (1) 4½" x 4½" (11.4 x 11.4cm) Fabric B square. Press with the shiny side down. This makes (1) Unit 5. Repeat to make a second Unit 5.

8. Finish the raw edges of each star with a decorative stitch, such as a blanket or satin stitch. Use matching threads. This completes (4) Unit 4 squares and (2) Unit 5 squares.

9. Sew (1) Unit 4 on each side of (1) Unit 5 to make (1) 4½" x 12½" (11.4 x 31.8cm) Unit 6. Repeat to make a second Unit 6.

Starburst Zipper Pouch

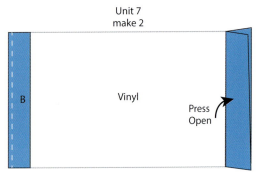
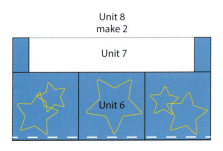

10. Place (2) 2½" x 6½" (6.4 x 16.5cm) Fabric B rectangles right sides together. Sandwich (1) piece of clear vinyl between, aligning the fabric pieces with a short edge of the vinyl. Sew together using a ¼" (6.4mm) seam allowance. Open the fabric and carefully press flat—**avoid touching the vinyl with the iron**. Repeat on the other short edge of the vinyl. Trim to 2½" x 6½" (6.4 x 16.5cm) to complete (1) Unit 7.

11. Repeat step 10 to make a second Unit 7.

12. Place (1) Unit 6 and (1) 4½" x 12½" (11.4 x 31.8cm) Fabric B rectangle right sides together. Sandwich (1) Unit 7 between, aligning the fabric pieces with a long edge of the vinyl. Sew together using a ¼" (6.4mm) seam allowance. Open the fabric and carefully press flat. This makes (1) Unit 8. Repeat to make a second Unit 8.

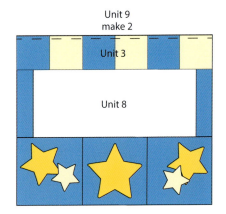
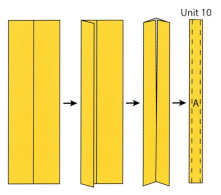

13. Place (1) Unit 3 and (1) 2½" x 12½" (6.4 x 31.8cm) Fabric B strip right sides together. Sandwich (1) Unit 8 between, aligning the fabric pieces with the remaining edge of the vinyl. Sew together using a ¼" (6.4mm) seam allowance. Open the fabric and carefully press flat. This makes (1) Unit 9. Repeat to make a second Unit 9.

14. Fold (1) 3" x 10" (7.6 x 25.4cm) Fabric A rectangle in half lengthwise and press. Open, fold each long edge to the creased centerline, and press. Fold the pressed fabric in half again. Press to make (1) ¾" x 10" (1.9 x 25.4cm) strip. Topstitch down both long sides, ⅛" (3.2mm) in from the edge, to make (1) Unit 10.

82 Quilting, Sewing & Appliqué: Essential Techniques for Beginners

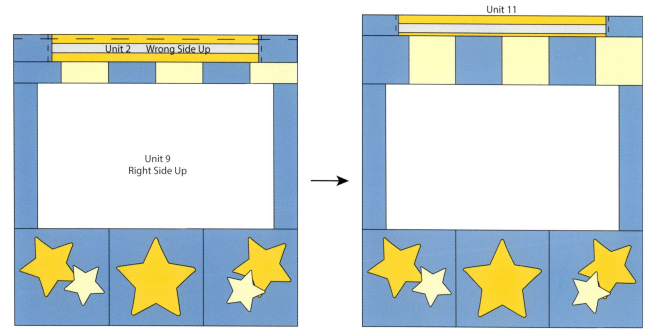

15. Place Unit 2 on top of (1) Unit 9 right sides together. Align along the top edge. Use a glue stick or clips to hold the pieces together. Using a zipper foot, sew the units together to make (1) Unit 11. Make sure to move the zipper head out of your way as you sew to make a straight seam.

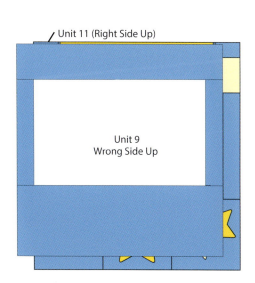

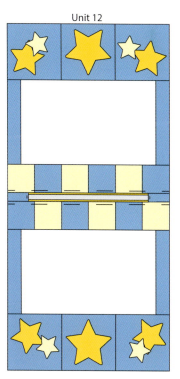

16. Place (1) Unit 9 on top of Unit 11, right sides together, aligning Unit 9's top edge with the zipper's raw edge. Glue or clip the pieces together. Use a zipper foot to sew the pieces together.

17. Open and press. Topstitch each edge next to the zipper to make (1) Unit 12.

Starburst Zipper Pouch

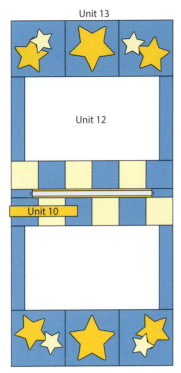

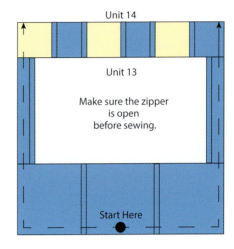

18. Fold Unit 10 in half lengthwise to form a Strap. Place the Strap onto Unit 12 as shown, aligning the raw edges. Pin or stitch baste the Strap to Unit 12 to make (1) Unit 13. Open the zipper halfway.

19. Fold the two halves of Unit 13, right sides together, to align the raw edges. Clip or pin together. Starting at the bottom center (represented by the dot), sew across the bottom and up the left side. Repeat on the right side. This makes (1) Unit 14. You can use a zigzag stitch over the raw edges of the bag if you choose.

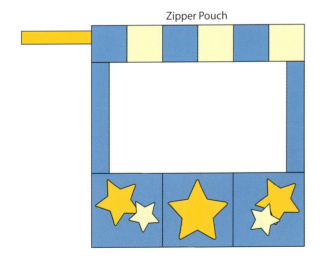

20. Turn Unit 14 right side out through the zipper opening. This completes the Starburst Zipper Pouch.

84   Quilting, Sewing & Appliqué: Essential Techniques for Beginners

Mini Daisy Pincushion

This adorable little pincushion is made from a Mini Daisy Block. It's a fun and easy project to create as a gift or to add to your creative space. After making one with the daisy template, you can experiment with designing your own artwork for the top of the pincushion.

FABRIC REQUIREMENTS:

Print—White Floral (A)	Fat Eighth
Solid—Bright Orange (B)	Fat Eighth
Solid—Bright Green (C)	Fat Eighth
Tonal—Violet (D)	Fat Eighth
Print—Lime Weave (E)	Fat Eighth

SUPPLY REQUIREMENTS:

- Mini Daisies templates (page 124)
- Fusible web
- 50wt matching cotton threads
- Basic sewing supplies and tools
- Walnut shells
- Stuffing
- Small funnel

CUTTING REQUIREMENTS:

Print—White Floral (Fabric A)
- (1) Daisy

Solid—Bright Orange (Fabric B)
- (1) Daisy Center

Solid—Bright Green (Fabric C)
- (1) 4½" x 4½" (11.4 x 11.4cm) square

Tonal—Violet (Fabric D)
- (1) Daisy Background

Print—Lime Weave (Fabric E)
- (1) 4½" x 4½" (11.4 x 11.4cm) square

Mini Daisy Pincushion 85

INSTRUCTIONS

1. Referring to Fusible Appliqué Basics (page 24), make the templates for the Mini Daisies Block as listed in the Cutting Requirements.

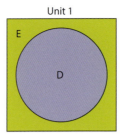

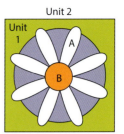

2. Refer to the Unit 1 diagram to arrange (1) Fabric D Daisy Background onto (1) 4½" x 4½" (11.4 x 11.4cm) Fabric E square. Press with the shiny side down. This makes (1) Unit 1.

3. Arrange and press (1) Fabric A Daisy onto (1) Unit 1. Arrange and press (1) Fabric B Daisy Center onto the unit. Finish the raw edges of each shape with a decorative stitch, such as a blanket or satin stitch. Use matching threads. This completes (1) Unit 2.

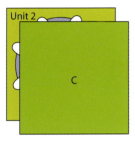

4. Place (1) 4½" x 4½" (11.4 x 11.4cm) Fabric C square on top of Unit 2, right sides together. Sew around the two pieces, leaving a 2" (5.1cm) opening for turning. This makes (1) Unit 3.

5. Turn Unit 3 right side out and press. Using a funnel, fill the unit with walnut shells to the desired fullness. Place a small amount of stuffing on top of the walnut shells to help keep them inside.

6. Hand stitch the opening closed. This completes the Mini Daisy Pincushion.

Mini Daisy Pincushion in Printed Fabric

This pattern can be reused with a variety of prints to make it your own.

FABRIC REQUIREMENTS:

Print—White Floral (A)	Fat Eighth
Print—Gold (B)	Fat Eighth
Print—Green-and-White Floral (C)	Fat Eighth
Solid—Red (D)	Fat Eighth
Print—Green-and-White Floral (E)	Fat Eighth

Putting It All Together

If you completed all 13 blocks with the intent to make the Inspire Quilt, in this section, we are going to go over how the blocks go together with the sashing and borders to make the quilt top. Then, we will go over layering and finishing the quilt. I hope you go out there and imagine great things, inspire others, keep dreaming big dreams, make others laugh, and smile with your new creations. Above all, keep on creating!

Building the Quilt Top

With all the blocks completed, it's time to bring them together to create the Inspire Quilt top. In this section, you'll follow step-by-step instructions to join the blocks with sashing, ensuring a clean and cohesive design.

By carefully assembling each row and adding sashing strips, you'll see your quilt take shape, transforming individual blocks into a unified composition. Take your time and enjoy this satisfying stage—your Inspire Quilt is almost ready for the next step!

FABRIC REQUIREMENTS:

Solid—Dark Yellow (A)
⅓ yard (30.5cm)

Tonal—Raspberry (B)
⅓ yard (30.5cm)

Solid—Royal Blue (C)
2¼ yards (205.7cm)

SUPPLY REQUIREMENTS:

- 50wt matching cotton threads
- Basic sewing supplies and tools
- (1) Imagine Block
- (1) Inspire Block
- (1) Sun Block
- (1) Laugh Block
- (1) Butterfly Block
- (1) Large Daisy Block
- (1) Create Block
- (1) Smile Block
- (1) Dream Block
- (1) Hearts Block
- (2) Starburst Blocks
- (1) Stars Block
- (1) Mini Daisies Block

CUTTING REQUIREMENTS:

Solid—Dark Yellow (Fabric A)
- (3) 2½" (6.4cm) x WOF strips

Tonal—Raspberry (Fabric B)
- (3) 2½" (6.4cm) x WOF strips

Solid—Royal Blue (Fabric C)
- (4) 3½" (8.9cm) x WOF rectangles. Sew the strips together end-to-end with diagonal seams. Subcut into:
  - (2) 3½" x 81½" (8.9 x 207cm) strips
- (4) 3½" (8.9cm) x WOF rectangles. Sew the strips together end-to-end with diagonal seams. Subcut into:
  - (2) 3½" x 74½" (8.9 x 189.2cm) strips
- (1) 5½" x 29½" (14 x 74.9cm) rectangle
- (2) 4½" x 29½" (11.4 x 74.9cm) rectangles
- (2) 3½" (8.9cm) x WOF rectangle. Subcut into:
  - (1) 3½" x 20½" (7.6 x 52.1cm) rectangle
  - (1) 3½" x 14½" (8.9 x 36.8cm) rectangle
  - (2) 3½" x 12½" (8.9 x 31.8cm) rectangle
- (2) 3" (7.6cm) x WOF rectangle. Subcut into:
  - (2) 3" x 27½" (7.6 x 69.9cm) rectangles
  - (2) 3" x 12½" (7.6 x 31.8cm) rectangles
- (6) 2½" (6.4cm) x WOF strips. Subcut into:
  - (1) 2½" x 27½" (6.4 x 69.9cm) strip
  - (3) 2½" x 24½" (6.4 x 62.2cm) strips
  - (4) 2½" x 20½" (6.4 x 52.1cm) strips
  - (1) 2½" x 12½" (6.4 x 31.8cm) strip

Quilting, Sewing & Appliqué: Essential Techniques for Beginners

Building the Quilt Top

INSTRUCTIONS

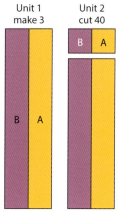
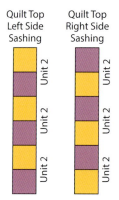

1. Sew (1) 2½" (6.4cm) x WOF Fabric B strip to the left side of (1) 2½" (6.4cm) x WOF Fabric A strip to make (1) Unit 1. Repeat to make (3) Unit 1 strips total. Cut (40) 2½" x 4½" (6.4 x 11.4cm) Unit 2 rectangles from strips.

2. Sew together (3) Unit 2 rectangles end-to-end in the order shown. This makes the Quilt Top Left Side Sashing. Repeat to make the Quilt Top Right Side Sashing.

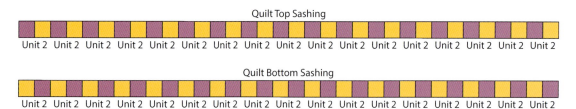

3. Sew together (17) Unit 2 rectangles end-to-end in the order shown. This makes the Quilt Top Sashing. Repeat to make the Quilt Bottom Sashing.

4. Assemble the Top Row using the (2) Starburst Blocks, (1) Imagine Block, and the sashing strips from steps 2 and 3. Remember to attach the Right Side and Left Side sashing strips before the Top and Bottom.

5. Join (1) 3" x 12½" (7.6 x 31.8cm) Fabric C rectangle to the top and to the bottom of the Inspire Block. This makes the 12½" x 45½" (31.8 x 115.6cm) Unit 1.

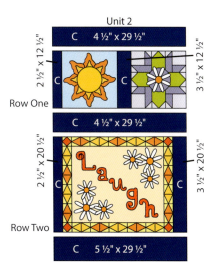

6. Join (1) 2½" x 12½" (6.4 x 31.8cm) Fabric C strip, (1) Sun Block, (1) 3½" x 12½" (7.6 x 31.8cm) Fabric C rectangle, and (1) Large Daisy Block, in that order from left to right. This makes Row One.

7. Join (1) 2½" x 20½" (6.4 x 52.1cm) Fabric C strip, (1) Laugh Block, and (1) 3½" x 20½" (7.6 x 52.1cm) Fabric C rectangle, in that order from left to right. This makes Row Two.

8. Join (1) 4½" x 29½" (11.4 x 74.9cm) Fabric C rectangle to the top and to the bottom of Row One. Attach the unit to Row Two and (1) 5½" x 29½" (14 x 74.9cm) Fabric C rectangle. This makes the 29½" x 45½" (74.9 x 115.6cm) Unit 2.

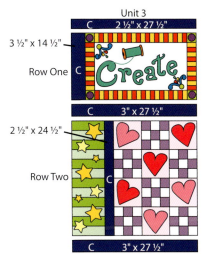

9. Join (1) 3½" x 14½" (7.6 x 36.8cm) Fabric C rectangle to the left side of (1) Create Block to make Row One. Join (1) Mini Stars Block, (1) 2½" x 24½" (6.4 x 62.2cm) Fabric C strip, and (1) Hearts Block, in that order from left to right, to make Row Two.

10. Join (1) 3" x 27½" (7.6 x 69.9cm) Fabric C rectangle to each side of Row Two. Attach the unit to Row One and (1) 2½" x 27½" (6.4 x 69.9cm) Fabric C strip. This makes the 27½" x 45½" (69.9 x 115.6cm) Unit 3.

11. Join (1) 2½" x 24½" (6.4 x 62.2cm) Fabric C strip to the top and to the bottom of (1) Smile Block. Sew (1) 2½" x 20½" (6.4 x 52.1cm) Fabric C strip to each side of the unit. This makes the 20½" x 28½" (52.1 x 72.4cm) Unit 4.

Building the Quilt Top

12. Join Unit 1, Unit 2, and Unit 3, in that order from left to right. This makes the 45½" x 68½" (115.6 x 174cm) Middle Row.

13. Join (1) Mini Daisies Block, (1) Unit 4, (1) Butterfly Block, (1) 2½" x 20½" (6.4 x 52.1cm) Fabric C strip, and (1) Dream Block, in that order from left to right. This makes the 20½" x 68½" (52.1 x 174cm) Bottom Row.

14. Join the Top Row, Middle Row, and Bottom Row, in that order from top to bottom. This makes the 81½" x 68½" (207 x 174cm) Center Block.

92   Quilting, Sewing & Appliqué: Essential Techniques for Beginners

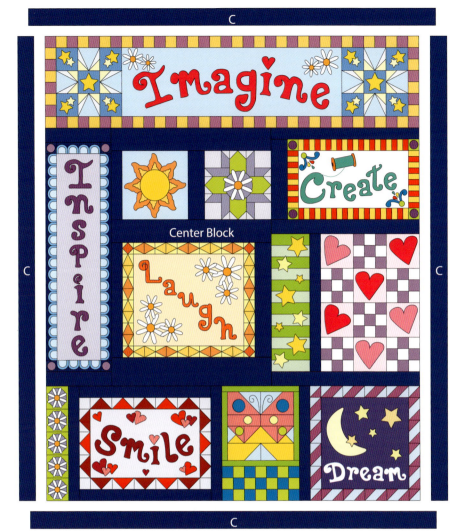

15. Attach (1) 3½" x 81½" (8.9 x 207cm) Fabric C strip to each side of the Center Block. Sew (1) 3½" x 74½" (8.9 x 189.2cm) Fabric C strip to the top and to the bottom of the Center Block. This completes the quilt top.

Imagine Quilt in Printed Fabric

All the blocks in this quilt can be made with a variety of prints to make it your own. Here, I'm only listing what is needed for the quilt outside of the blocks. But use this as inspiration for what can be done.

FABRIC REQUIREMENTS:

Solid—Light Green (A)	⅓ yard (30.5cm)
Print—Dark Teal Geometric (B)	⅓ yard (30.5cm)
Print—Teal Floral (C)	2¼ yards (205.7cm)

Building the Quilt Top

Making the Quilt Sandwich

Before you can quilt your masterpiece, you need to assemble the foundation that holds it all together—the quilt sandwich. This crucial step involves layering the quilt top, batting, and backing to create a stable and well-balanced piece ready for stitching. A properly prepared quilt sandwich ensures smooth quilting, prevents shifting, and enhances the overall look of your finished quilt.

Whether you're working on a small wall hanging or a full-sized bed quilt, mastering this technique will help you achieve professional-looking results. Let's get started on building the perfect foundation for your quilting success!

FABRIC REQUIREMENTS:
Quilt Back
 5½ yards (502.9cm)

SUPPLY REQUIREMENTS:
- 50wt matching cotton threads
- Basic sewing supplies and tools
- (1) 82" x 95" (208.3 x 241.3cm) piece of batting
- Size 0 safety pins

Watch a video tutorial on quilt backing.

1. Trim the selvage edges off the quilt back fabric. Cut the backing fabric into two pieces that each measure 99" (251.5cm) x WOF.

2. Place the two pieces of fabric right sides together. Sew down each long side of the layered fabrics. Using a pair of scissors, cut through the top layer—and only the top layer—of the sewn fabrics straight down the middle.

94 Quilting, Sewing & Appliqué: Essential Techniques for Beginners

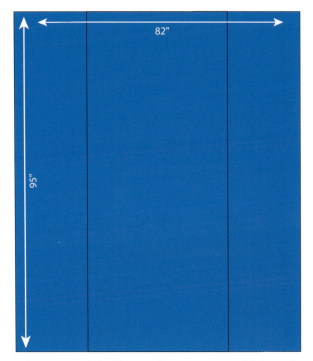

3. Flip out each half to make one piece of fabric that measures approximately 88" x 99" (223.5 x 251.5cm). Trim the fabric to measure 82" x 95" (208.3 x 241.3cm) for the backing piece. Press the seams and the quilt backing fabric.

4. Press the quilt top to remove any wrinkles.

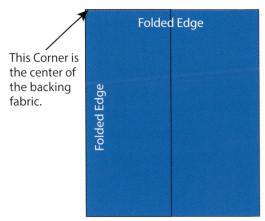

5. Fold the backing fabric in half wrong sides together. Fold again so the backing fabric is in quarters. Repeat with the batting and quilt top.

6. Lay the backing fabric onto a flat surface with the folded center point in the middle of the table.

7. Carefully unfold the backing fabric so the wrong side is facing up.

Tip: Use binder clips to hold the backing fabric to the flat surface, keeping it from sliding around.

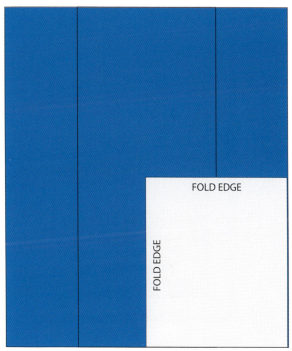

8. Place the folded batting on top of the backing, aligning the folded center point of the batting with the center of the backing. Carefully unfold the batting and smooth it out on top of the backing fabric.

Making the Quilt Sandwich

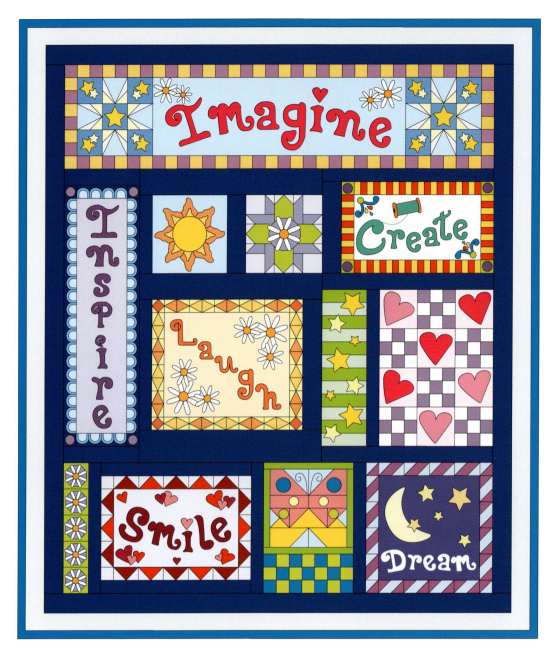

9. Repeat step 8 to position the quilt top on top of and in the center of the batting. Check each side of the layered pieces to make sure the batting and backing are both approximately 4" (10.2cm) longer than the quilt top.

10. Smooth out all three layers to make sure there are no wrinkles on each of the layers.

11. Using safety pins, pin through the three layers about 4"–6" (10.2–15.2cm) apart to baste the sandwich together. Start in the middle of the layered pieces. Your quilt sandwich is now ready to quilt.

Quilting the Quilt

Most quilt patterns will tell you to quilt your project as desired because how you stitch your quilt is such a personal choice. This can be very overwhelming for beginners, so here are some guidelines to get you started. Please note that you can be as creative with your quilt as you wish. Play with thread colors, stitching designs, and styles to make the quilting your own.

SUPPLY REQUIREMENTS:
- 50wt matching cotton threads
- Basic sewing supplies and tools
- Walking foot
- Free motion foot

1. Using a walking foot, complete all the straight stitching (stitch-in-the-ditch), which is mostly the seams formed from piecing. Also sew around the borders and sashing. This will hold the layers together and add some structure to your quilt.

2. Add free motion quilting, which is like drawing with threads. Drop the feed dogs on the sewing machine and switch the foot to a free motion foot. Start in the middle and work out to each edge of the quilt. Remove the safety pins from each area that you quilt, as quilting secures the layers.

3. For our sample, we switched the thread colors to match each block and stitched around the fusible appliqué shapes to make them pop. Then we doodled in the background to fill in the open areas.

4. Once the quilt sandwich is finished, use a ruler and rotary cutter to trim the batting and backing even with the quilt top.

Fill in the open spaces of a quilt project with stitching. Quilting holds the layers together and adds a subtle design.

Tip: There are so many videos and books available to teach you about different ways to quilt. I recommend referencing some of these for other wonderful ideas on how to quilt your project.

Binding the Quilt

These instructions show you how to put a binding on a quilt completely by machine. With our technique, the binding is sewn to the back of the quilt first and then turned to the front of the quilt to be stitched in place with a blind hem stitch. This is a quick and easy alternative to hand sewing a binding in place.

Watch a video tutorial on binding.

SUPPLY REQUIREMENTS:
- 50wt matching cotton threads
- Basic sewing supplies and tools
- 2½" (6.4cm) binding ruler or a ruler with a 45-degree edge (available on my website)
- Pins

FABRIC REQUIREMENTS:
Tonal—Iris (D)   ⅔ yard (61cm)

CUTTING REQUIREMENTS:
Tonal—Iris (Fabric D)
- (8) 2½" (6.4cm) x WOF strips

FIGURING YARDAGE AMOUNT AND STRIPS REQUIRED

For this quilt, we have already listed the binding strips needed. Binding strips are typically 2½" (6.4cm) wide, but the number of strips depends on the size of the project. Here is the way to figure out how many strips of fabric you would need for any project you make in the future. Included are examples matching this quilt, so you can follow why this amount is recommended.

1. Add up all four sides of the quilt and add 12" (30.5cm).
   - Example: 74" x 87" (188 x 221cm) quilt.
   - 74" (188cm) + 74" (188cm) + 87" (221cm) + 87" (221cm) + 12" (30.5cm) = 334" (848.4cm)

2. Divide this number by the width of fabric (WOF) measurement.
   - In this case, we will use 42" (106.7cm).
   - 334 ÷ 42 = 7.9

3. Round this number up to get the number of binding strips needed.
   - 7.9 rounds up to 8 strips. You will need 8 strips, measuring 2½" (6.4cm) x WOF, for binding.

4. To figure out the yardage, multiply the number of strips by the binding strip width.
   - 8 x 2½" (6.4cm) = 20" (50.8cm) of binding fabric is needed for this quilt.

I recommended cutting ⅔ yards (24" [61cm]) of Fabric D because of how fabric is typically sold at most shops. Since 20" (50.8cm) is just over ½ yard (18" [45.7cm]), the next closest standard cut is ⅔ yard. Rounding up ensures you have enough fabric to work with, accounting for variations in cutting, shrinkage, or adjustments needed during your project. It's always better to have a little extra fabric rather than risk running short!

Quilting, Sewing & Appliqué: Essential Techniques for Beginners

ATTACHING THE BINDING

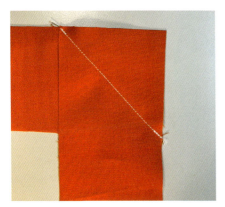

1. Lay (2) 2½" (6.4cm) x WOF Fabric D strips right sides together. Arrange the ends together and at a perpendicular angle. Sew across the diagonal and trim the excess fabric.

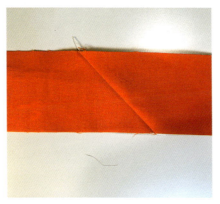

2. Flip the top strip over and press open. Continue adding to the binding strip with the remaining (6) strips.

3. Fold the long binding strip in half lengthwise with wrong sides together. Press this strip along the folded edge. **Note:** This strip is blue in the remaining instructions.

4. Position the binding on the back of the quilt, starting about halfway down one side. Line up the raw edges. Using a walking foot, start sewing approximately 8" (20.3cm) down from the top edge of the binding strip. Use a ¼" (6.4mm) seam allowance.

5. Sew until you are ¼" (6.4mm) away from the bottom edge. Rotate the quilt so the sewn binding edge is now on top and the adjacent side to be sewn is on the right.

6. Flip the binding strip straight up. This will create a 45-degree fold.

Note: If you are attaching the binding by hand, sew the binding strip to the front of the quilt instead of the back.

Binding the Quilt

7. Put your thumb on top of the 45-degree angle. Fold the binding strip straight down to make a French-fold corner. If needed, straighten the folded corner so it is square to the quilt corner.

8. Start sewing at the top edge of the quilt over the French-fold corner. Continue down the binding, stopping ¼" (6.4mm) from the bottom edge.

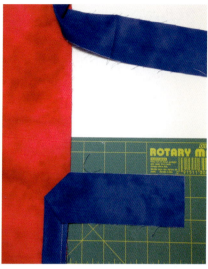

9. Repeat steps 5–8 to attach the binding to all sides of the quilt. Stop 6"–8" (15.2–20.3cm) away from the starting point.

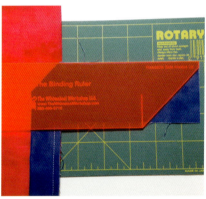

10. Place the binding ruler (or 45-degree ruler) on top of the binding strip. Align it with the quilt top and one end of the binding strip as shown. Cut the end of the binding strip following the angle of the ruler, maintaining a short straight edge at the top.

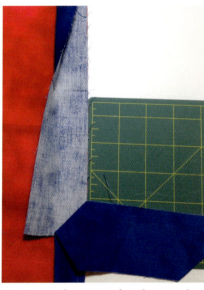

11. Bring the upper binding end down. Open the strip flat, wrong side facing up.

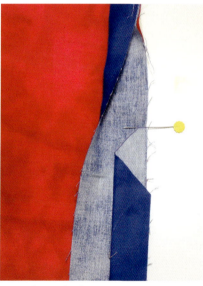

12. Place the lower strip inside the upper strip. It should be folded with the right side up. Place a straight pin into the upper strip where the lower strip meets. Only put the pin through the upper binding strip—not the quilt sandwich or lower binding strip.

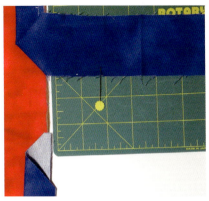  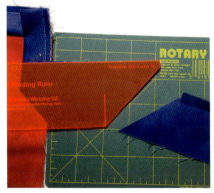

13. Fold out the upper binding strip onto a small cutting mat. Keep it opened flat, wrong side down.

14. Place the ruler on top of the upper binding strip. Align the end of the 45-degree angle with the pin.

15. Cut the binding strip at the top straight end first, marking the length of the binding strip. Remove the straight pin and cut the angle following the binding ruler.

16. Align the top and bottom strips, right sides together, along the two angled ends. Sew them together using a ¼" (6.4mm) seam allowance.

17. Refold the sewn binding, aligning the raw edges with the quilt's raw edges. Finish sewing the binding in place.

18. Fold the binding over the raw edge of the quilt to the front of the quilt. Set your sewing machine to stitch a blind hem stitch about ⅛" (3.2mm) wide and ⅛" (3.2mm) long. Using invisible thread or matching thread, stitch the binding in place.

Binding the Quilt 101

Templates

Imagine Block and Pillow

Templates Reversed for Fusible Appliqué

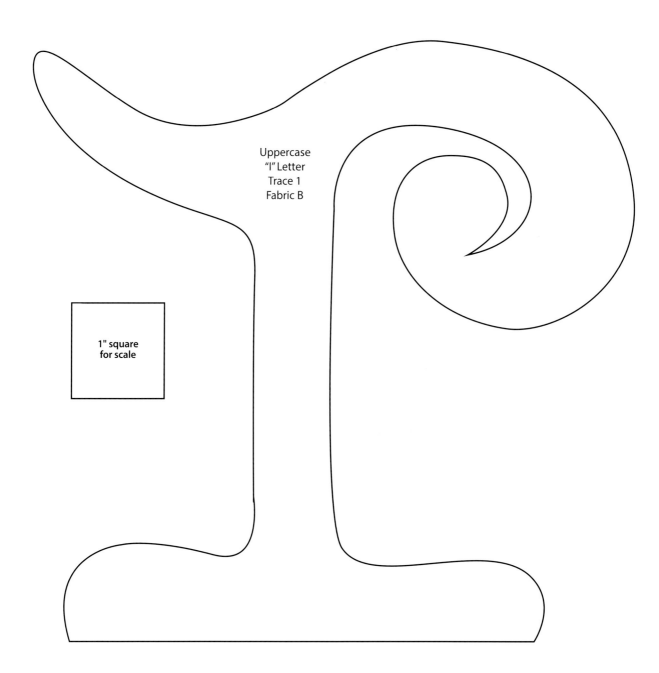

Uppercase "I" Letter
Trace 1
Fabric B

1" square for scale

Imagine Block and Pillow
Templates Reversed for Fusible Appliqué

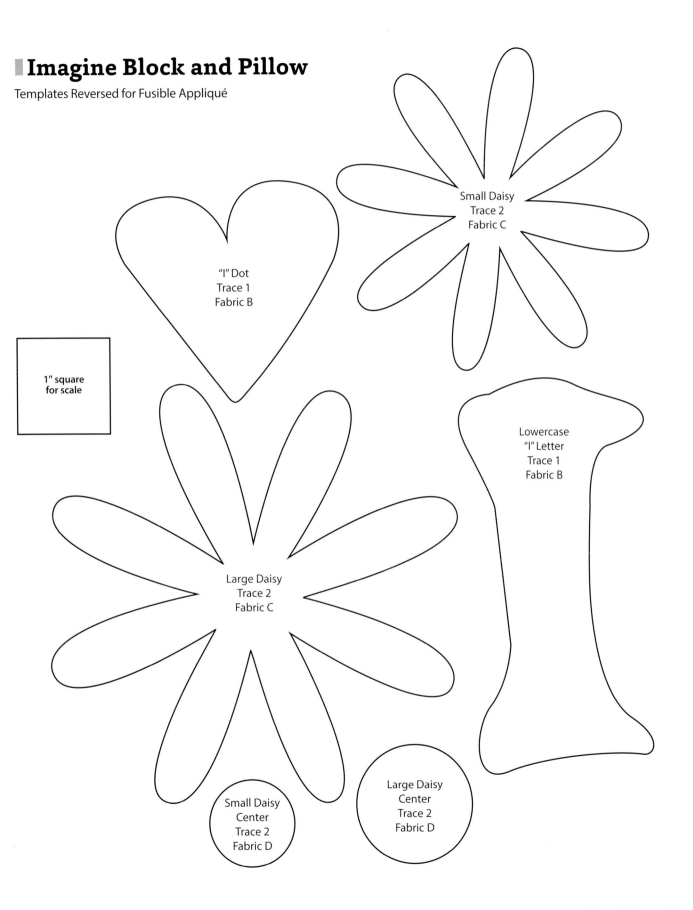

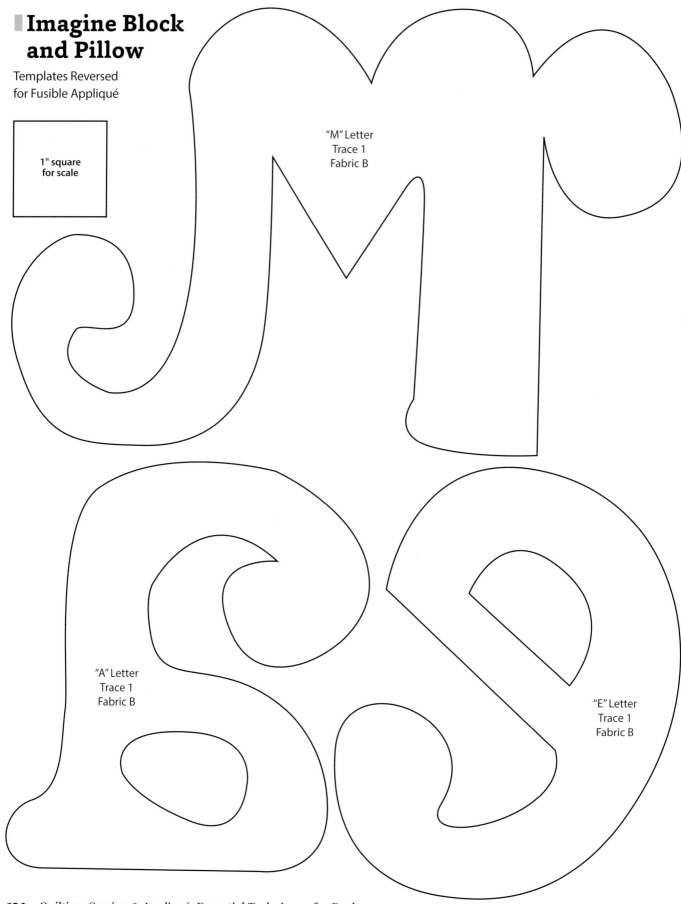

Imagine Block and Pillow
Templates Reversed for Fusible Appliqué

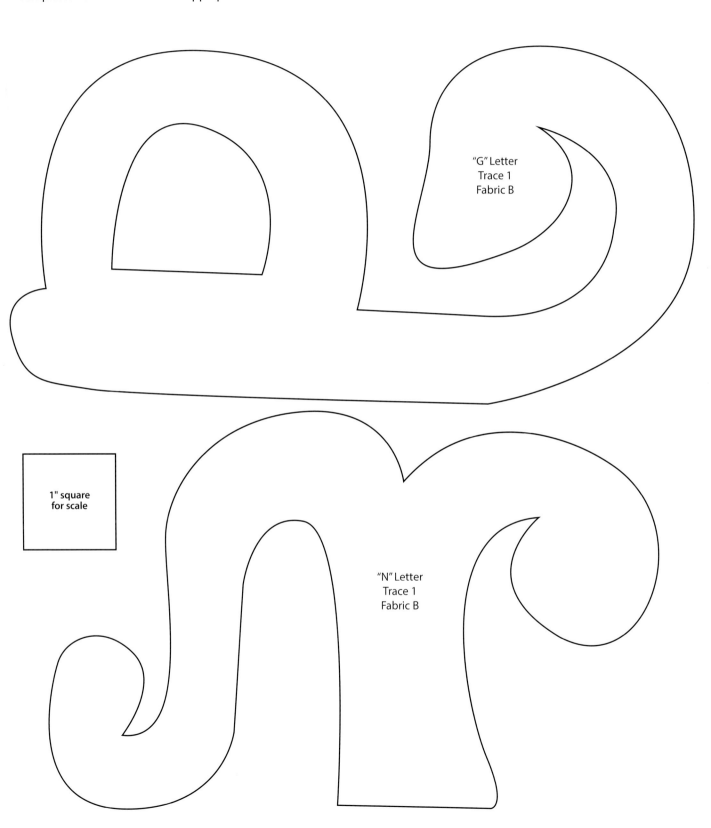

Inspire Block
Templates Reversed for Fusible Appliqué

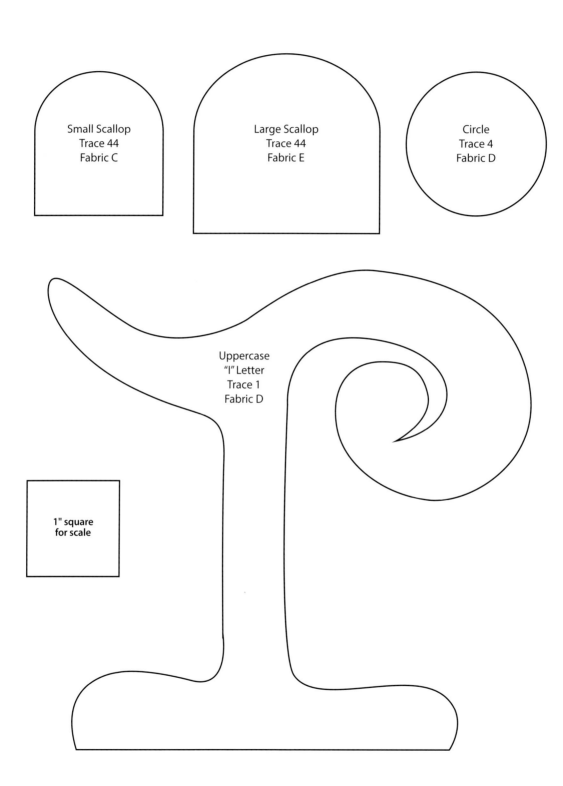

106   Quilting, Sewing & Appliqué: Essential Techniques for Beginners

Inspire Block
Templates Reversed for Fusible Appliqué

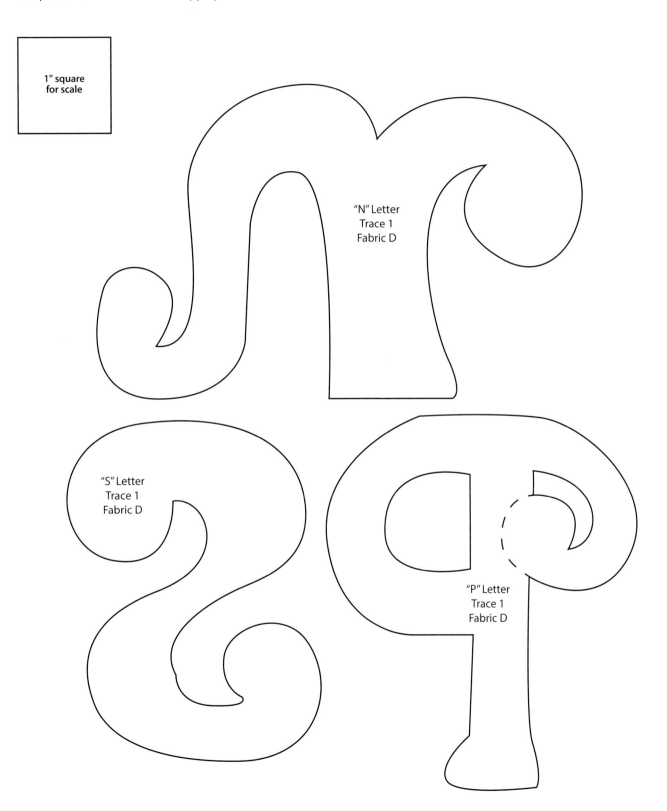

Templates 107

Inspire Block

100% Templates Reversed for Fusible Appliqué

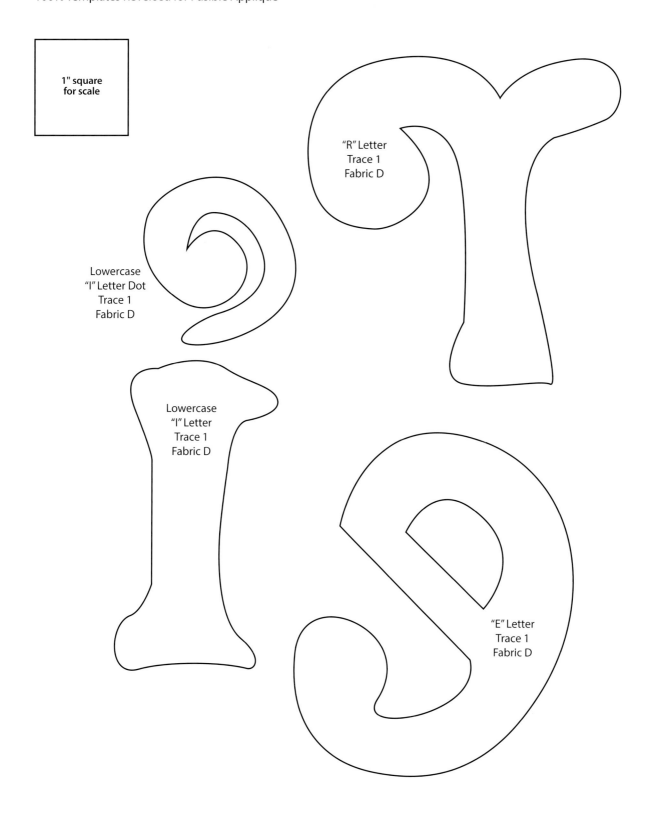

Sun Block
Templates Reversed for Fusible Appliqué

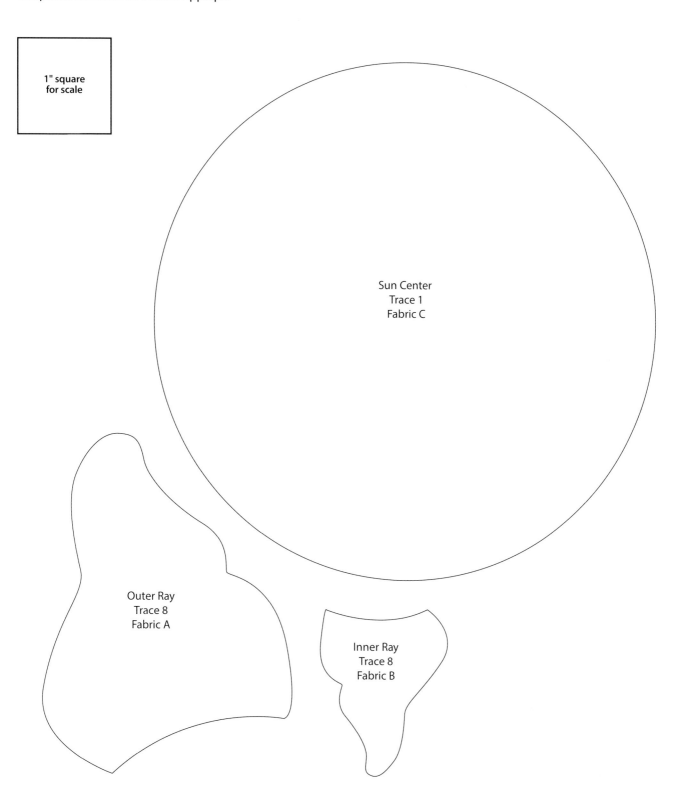

1" square for scale

Sun Center
Trace 1
Fabric C

Outer Ray
Trace 8
Fabric A

Inner Ray
Trace 8
Fabric B

Templates **109**

Sun Basket

Templates Reversed for Fusible Appliqué

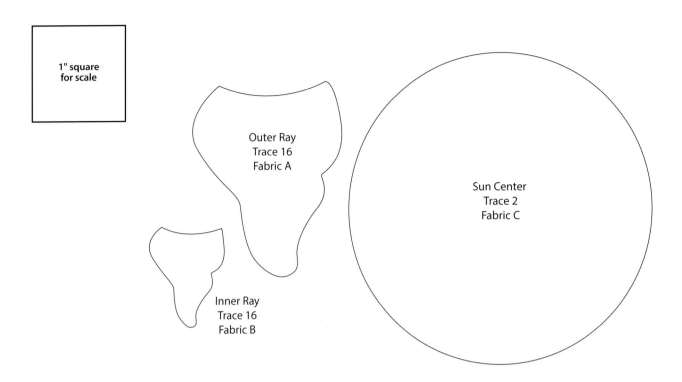

Laugh Block and Runner

Templates Reversed for Fusible Appliqué

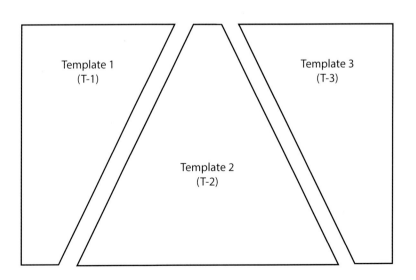

110   Quilting, Sewing & Appliqué: Essential Techniques for Beginners

Laugh Block and Runner
Templates Reversed for Fusible Appliqué

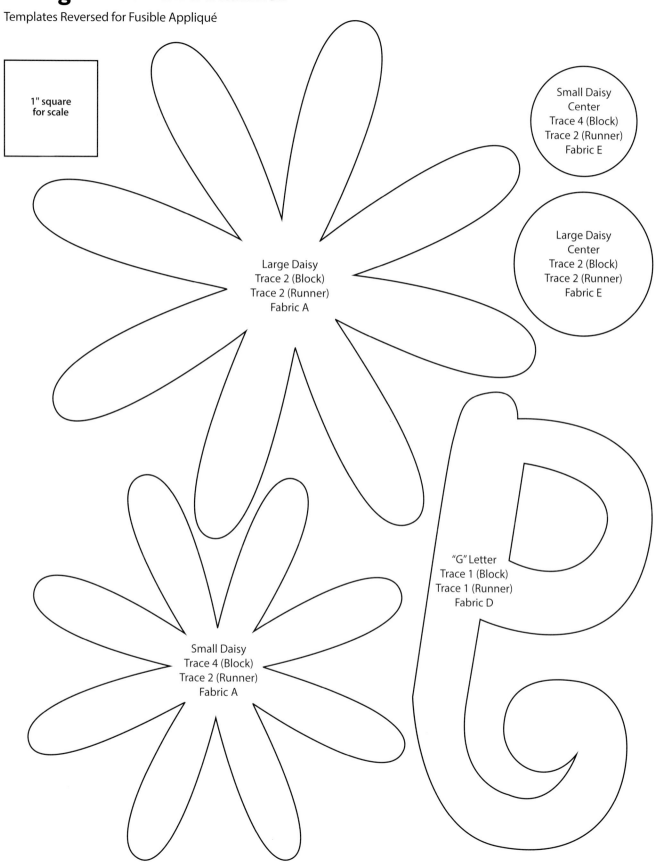

Templates 111

Laugh Block and Runner
Templates Reversed for Fusible Appliqué

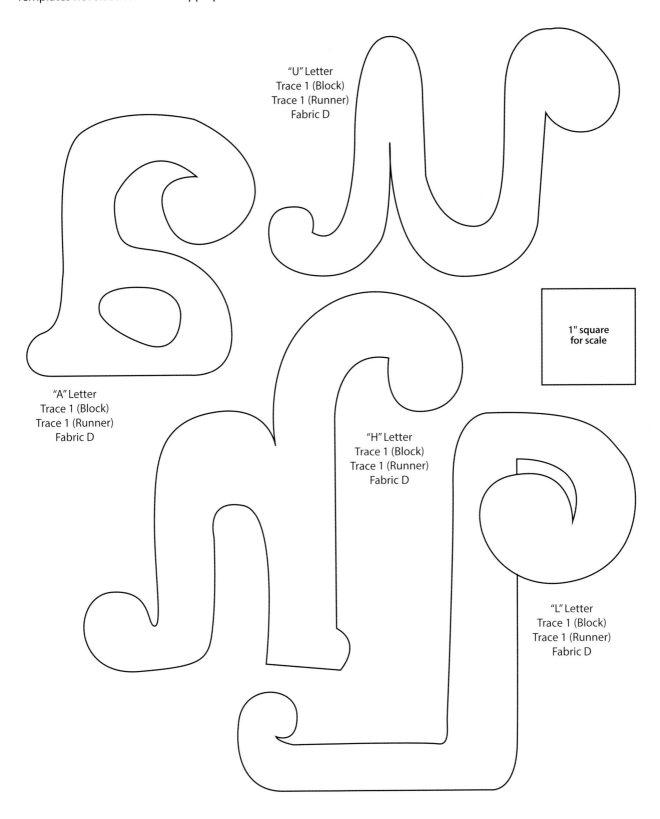

Butterfly Block
Templates Reversed for Fusible Appliqué

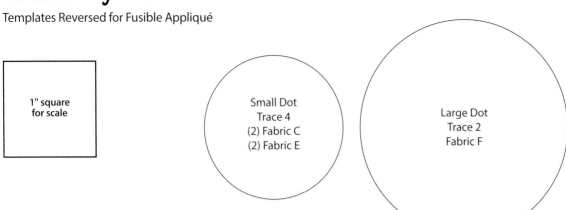

Large Daisy Block
Templates Reversed for Fusible Appliqué

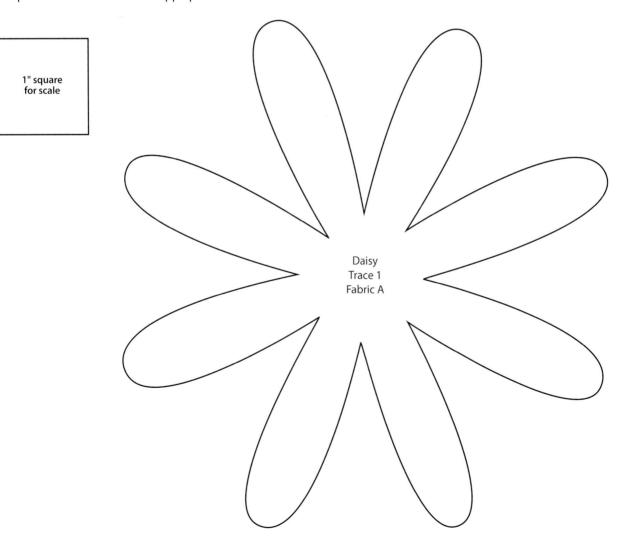

Templates 113

Large Daisy Block

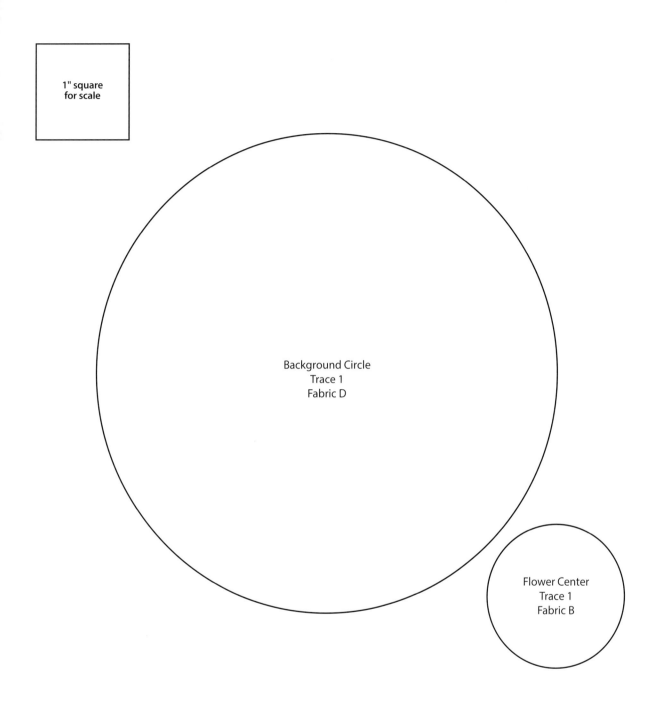

1" square for scale

Background Circle
Trace 1
Fabric D

Flower Center
Trace 1
Fabric B

Create Block
Templates Reversed for Fusible Appliqué

Create Block
Templates Reversed for Fusible Appliqué

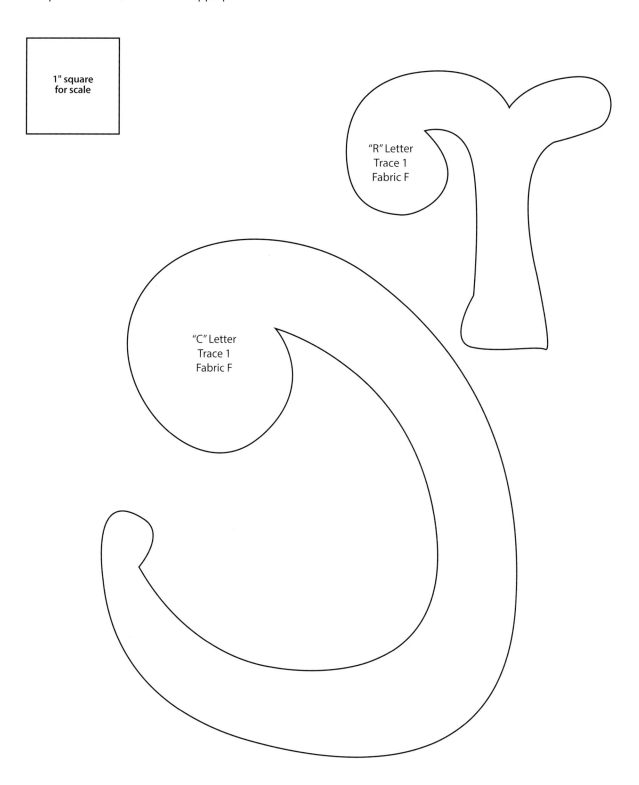

1" square for scale

"R" Letter
Trace 1
Fabric F

"C" Letter
Trace 1
Fabric F

Smile Block
Templates Reversed for Fusible Appliqué

Smile Block
Templates Reversed for Fusible Appliqué

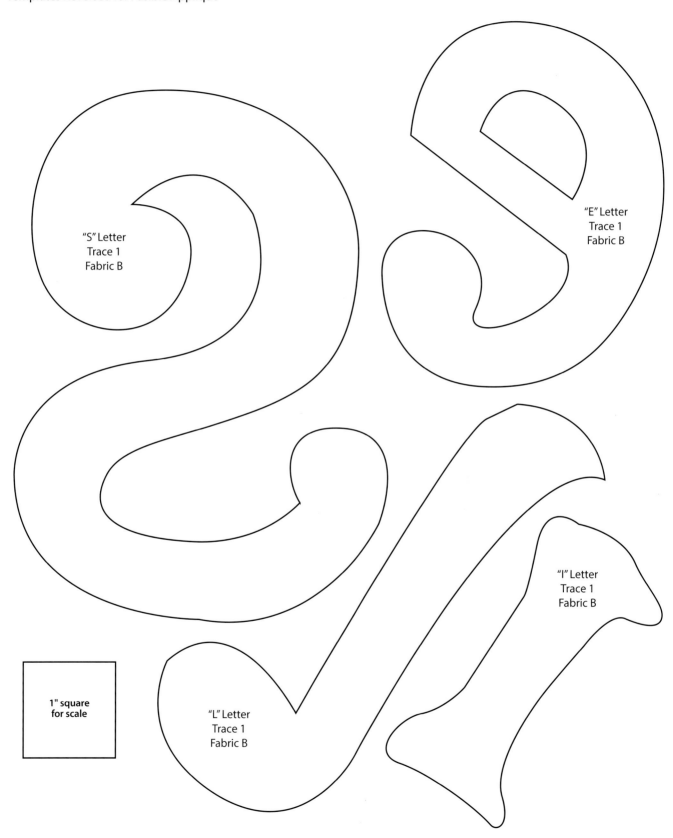

118 Quilting, Sewing & Appliqué: Essential Techniques for Beginners

Dream Block and Pillow
Templates Reversed for Fusible Appliqué

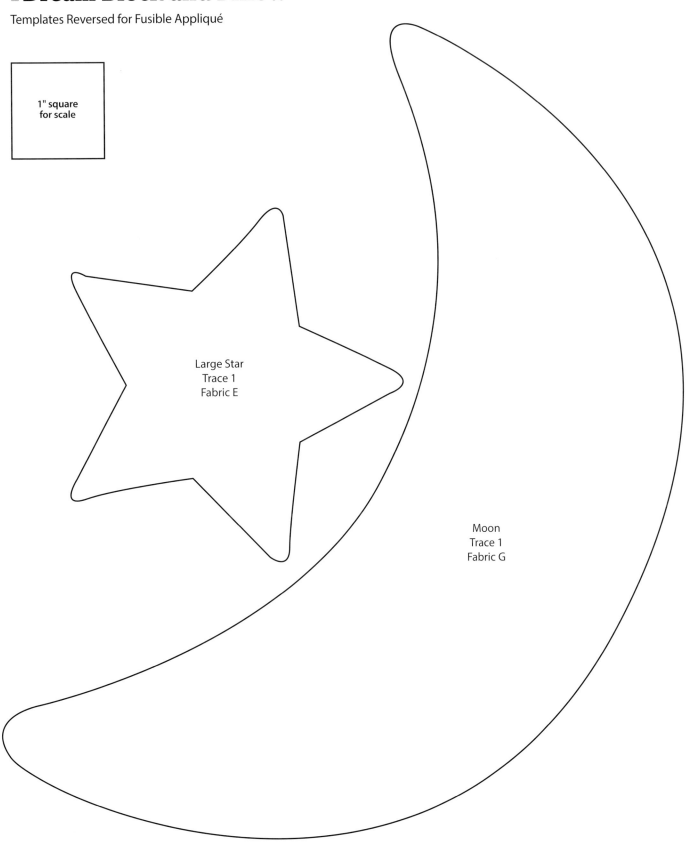

1" square for scale

Large Star
Trace 1
Fabric E

Moon
Trace 1
Fabric G

Templates 119

Dream Block and Pillow
Templates Reversed for Fusible Appliqué

120 Quilting, Sewing & Appliqué: Essential Techniques for Beginners

Hearts Block

Templates Reversed for Fusible Appliqué

Starburst Block
Templates Reversed for Fusible Appliqué

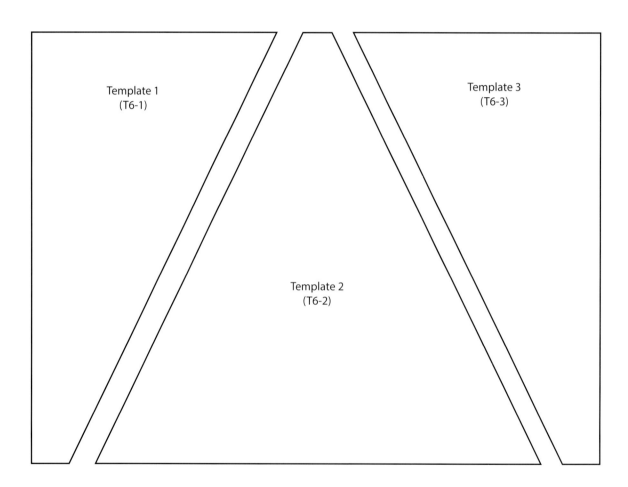

Starburst Block and Pouch

Templates Reversed for Fusible Appliqué
Note: Double the Block amount if using for the Inspire Quilt.

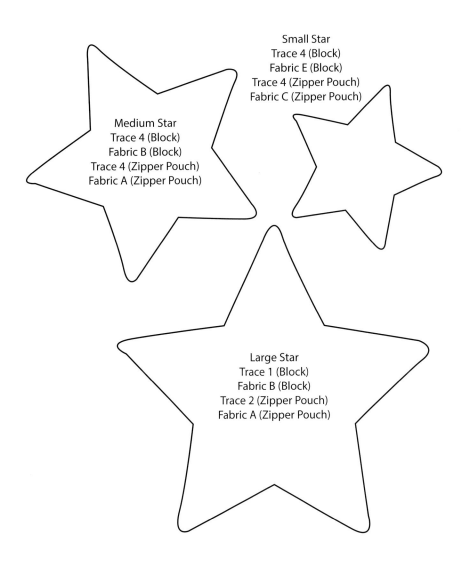

1" square for scale

Small Star
Trace 4 (Block)
Fabric E (Block)
Trace 4 (Zipper Pouch)
Fabric C (Zipper Pouch)

Medium Star
Trace 4 (Block)
Fabric B (Block)
Trace 4 (Zipper Pouch)
Fabric A (Zipper Pouch)

Large Star
Trace 1 (Block)
Fabric B (Block)
Trace 2 (Zipper Pouch)
Fabric A (Zipper Pouch)

Stars Block / Mini Daisies Block and Pincushion

Templates Reversed for Fusible Appliqué

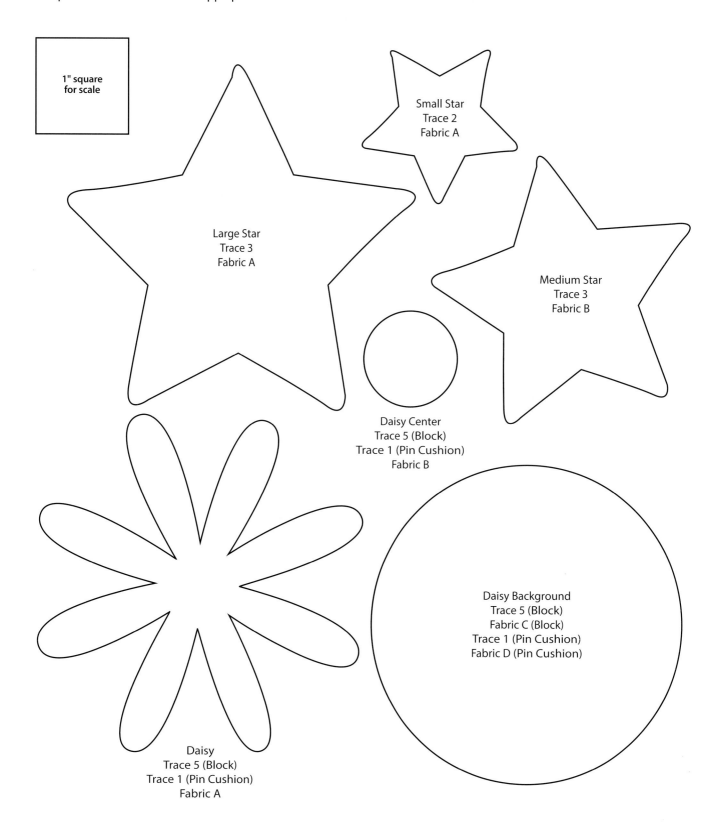

124   Quilting, Sewing & Appliqué: Essential Techniques for Beginners

Acknowledgments

Creating this book has been a journey, filled with creativity, dedication, and the unwavering support of so many wonderful people. I am incredibly grateful to all of you who played a role in bringing this project to life.

This book is dedicated to my dad, Doug Sauer. At the very start of this project, while visiting, he helped me cut and prepare all the pieces, setting everything in motion. Sadly, we lost him about halfway through the writing of this book, but his presence never left. Each time I moved to the next section, I would see his handwriting and be reminded of the incredible man who encouraged me at every step. His fingerprints are all over this book, and I hope everyone is lucky enough to have the unwavering support I had in him.

To my husband and business partner, Matthew—there is no one else I would want by my side through this crazy, wonderful life we've built together. As my partner in The Whimsical Workshop, you have been there every step of the way, supporting my creative vision, helping navigate the ups and downs, and making sure our dreams become reality. Beyond business, you have been my rock, my biggest cheerleader, and my greatest partner in life. I couldn't do this without you, and I wouldn't want to.

A huge thank-you to B'nea Pulve for her incredible quilting talent. Your ability to bring my designs to life, even on a short deadline, is nothing short of amazing. I couldn't have asked for a more skilled and dedicated collaborator.

To Darren Mulqueen, thank you for requesting the original design that set this entire journey in motion. Your trust in my work, along with the space and support you gave me to fully realize my vision, has been invaluable.

I also want to express my appreciation to everyone who has inspired, encouraged, and contributed to this book—whether through quilting, feedback, or simply cheering me on along the way. The quilting community is truly a special one, and I am honored to be a part of it.

Finally, to my readers—thank you for sharing in this passion. May this book inspire you to create, explore, and find joy in every stitch.

Happy quilting!

About the Author

Heidi Pridemore was born and raised in Rochester, New York, and earned a bachelor's degree in industrial design from the Rochester Institute of Technology. She began her career as a product designer for fabric companies in 2000 and launched her own line of quilt patterns in 2002. By 2005, she cofounded The Whimsical Workshop LLC, where she serves as the lead designer, creating vibrant and whimsical quilts known for their playful style and clear instructions.

Heidi collaborates with national fabric companies, including Island Batik, designing fabric collections and project sheets. Her work has been featured in popular quilting magazines, such as *Quiltmaker*, *McCall's Quick Quilts*, *The Quilter*, and *Quilts*. As an accomplished author, she has written books covering quilting, pop-up paper structures, and fabric jewelry.

In addition to her design work, Heidi runs The Whimsical Workshop's retail website, www.thewhimsicalworkshop.com, where customers can find a wide selection of quilt patterns, fabric kits, fabric collections, books, and exclusive designs. The site also features helpful resources for quilters and crafters of all skill levels.

Beyond her business, Heidi is an Aurifilosopher and BERNINA Ambassador, representing Aurifil Threads. She travels extensively to trade shows, gives lectures, and leads workshops. She also shares her expertise on YouTube through The Whimsical Workshop. When not traveling, she enjoys life in Arizona with her husband and design partner, Matthew.

About the Tech Editor

Lorelai Kuecker started her quilting journey at the age of 12. From that day forward, it has been a whirlwind of classes, projects, and YouTube tutorials. In three short years, she has quickly become known for her custom quilting talents and her quilted garments and bags. Lorelai has won awards at the 2023 Kansas City Regional Quilt Festival, the 2024 Branson AQS Quilt Show, and has had a quilt displayed in the 2024 Houston International Quilt Festival.

She was featured in the June 2023 edition of *Fons and Porter Quick and Easy Quilts* and has had the honor of collaborating with The Ruby Start Society, Northcott Fabrics, and the Quilted Cow. She has been asked to present her Trunk Show at the 2025 Branson AQS Quilt Show and will be teaching youth-oriented classes at the 2025 Kansas City Regional Quilt Festival. She is also writing a book for Fox Chapel Publishing that will come out in 2026.

When she isn't working on her dual-credit classes, she plays French horn in the Kansas City Youth Orchestra and is a member of the CenterStage Players theatre group, where her favorite role has been Cinderella in the production of *Into the Woods, Jr.*

Index

A
acrylic ruler, 13
appliqué pressing sheet, 18
appliqué supplies, 18

B
basket, 69
batiks, 16
batting, 19
binding, 98
butterfly, 38

C
checkerboard block, 55
checkerboard, 38
cutting mat, 13

D
daisies, 28, 35
   large, 42
   mini, 63, 85
diagonal striped edging, 51
diamond edging, 35

E
erasable marking pen, 14

F
fabric shears, 13
fabrics, 16
   solid or single-color, 17
fiberfill, 19
fusible appliqué basics, 24
   tips, 24–25
fusible fleece, 20
fusible foam, 20
fusible web, 18

G
glue stick, temporary, 14

H
half-square triangle basics, 21
   variation, 58
hearts, 48, 55
HST basics, 21
   variation, 58

I
iron and ironing board, 12

M
marker, permanent, 18
marking pen, erasable, 14
milliners needles, 15
moon, 51

N
needles
   hand-sewing, 15
   milliners, 15

O
open-toe presser foot, 18

P
paper scissors, 13
permanent marker, 18
piecing basics, 23
pillow, 66, 76
pin cushion, 14
pincushion, 85
presser foot, open-toe, 18
pressing sheet, for appliqué, 18
prints, 16

Q
quilt, 87
quilt backing (video, QR code), 94
quilt binding (video, QR code), 98
quilt cottons, 16
quilting, 97
quilt sandwich, making the, 94

R
rotary cutter, 13

S
scallop edging, 30
scissors, 13
seam allowance
   how to sew a quarter-inch (video, QR code), 21
seam ripper, 15
sewing clips, 14
sewing machine, 12
stabilizers, 19
stars, 51, 58, 61, 80
straight pins, 14
striped edging, 45
stuffing, 19
sun, 33, 69

T
table runner, 73
thread colors, picking, 17
thread snips, 13
threads, 17

V
videos
   beginner quilting series (QR code), 6
   how to sew a quarter-inch seam allowance (QR code), 21
   quilt backing (QR code), 94
   binding (QR code), 98
vinyl, 20

W
wadding, 19

Z
zipper pouch, 80